THE YOUNG
OXFORD
LIBRARY OF
SCIENCE

Mind and Body

Brenda Walpole

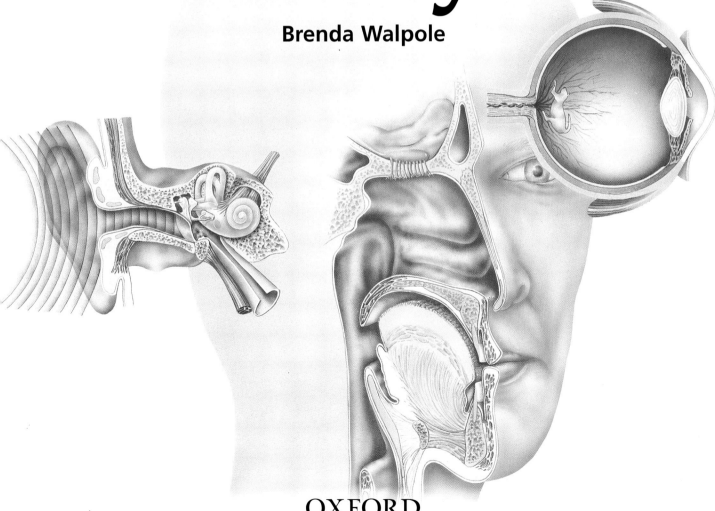

OXFORD
UNIVERSITY PRESS

OXFORD

UNIVERSITY PRESS

Great Clarendon Street, Oxford OX2 6DP

Oxford University Press is a department of the University of Oxford.
It furthers the University's objective of excellence in research, scholarship,
and education by publishing worldwide in

Oxford New York

Auckland Bangkok Buenos Aires Cape Town Chennai
Dar es Salaam Delhi Hong Kong Istanbul Karachi
Kolkata Kuala Lumpur Madrid Melbourne Mexico City Mumbai
Nairobi São Paulo Shanghai Singapore Taipei Tokyo Toronto

with an associated company in Berlin

Oxford is a registered trade mark of Oxford University Press
in the UK and in certain other countries

British Library Cataloguing in Publication Data available

Hardback ISBN 0-19-910938-9
Paperback ISBN 0-19-910939-7

1 3 5 7 9 10 8 6 4 2

Designed and typeset by Full Steam Ahead
Printed in Malaysia.

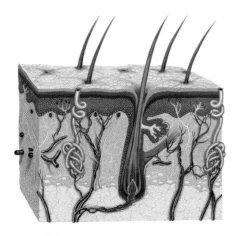

CONTENTS

Human beings 4

Perfect protection 7

The bare bones 8

Food for life 10

Digesting food 12

Chemical control 14

Balancing water 15

Every breath you take 16

Our transport system 18

Chemical messengers 20

The nervous system 22

Sensing the world 24

All in the mind 26

Word of mouth 28

In your genes 29

A new life begins 30

Growing up 32

Fighting disease 34

Keeping healthy 36

Sneezes and diseases 37

Coping with cancer 39

Treating illness 40

Looking inside the body 43

Delicate operations 44

Glossary 46

Index 47

Acknowledgements 48

HUMAN BEINGS

▶ The skeleton of Lucy. This almost complete skeleton was named *Australopithecus afarensis* after the Afar region of Ethiopia where it was found.

In 1974, the remains of a 3-million-year-old female skeleton were discovered in Ethiopia. Scientists called her Lucy, and she forms the closest link we have between apes and human beings.

Lucy was an Australopithecine – a southern ape. The evidence from Lucy's skeleton suggests that, unlike the apes, she walked upright, just as we do. Remains of other Australopithecines have been found in Kenya, Tanzania and South Africa. Their teeth, jaws and many other features are very similar to our own.

Early humans

Scientists have found many other fossil remains of our ancient relations in Africa. *Homo habilis* ('handyman') flourished over a million years after Lucy, in East Africa. *Homo habilis* walked upright, was probably about the same size as a 12-year-old boy is today, and had a larger brain than the Lucy. *Homo habilis* were probably the first creatures to make tools, which is why they are known as 'handy'.

Homo erectus

Homo erectus means 'upright man'. These people lived about a million years ago. They walked upright and used tools. They also used fire to keep warm, which made it possible for them to live in cooler climates. Their remains have been found near Beijing in China and in Europe.

Homo sapiens

About 200,000 years ago a new group of humans evolved in Africa and moved north. These were *Homo sapiens* ('wise man'), and they were very similar to us. They lived in groups, and hunted large animals such as deer and mammoths. We know they

▼ Humans developed through a number of stages over the last 3 million years. Here are the main stages.

Lucy (Australopithecine) probably looked something like this. She walked upright, but probably not with the same kind of stride as we do.

Homo habilis used cutting, scraping and hammering tools.

Homo erectus people were the first to use fire.

| 3 mya (million years ago) | 2 mya | 1.5 mya |

communicated with each other from the pictures and symbols they drew.

Neanderthals

Neanderthal people were a group of *Homo sapiens* who lived in Europe and the Middle East between 80,000 and 30,000 years ago. They were probably the first people to bury their dead. Scientists think that the Neanderthals are more closely related to us than any of the other early humans that have been found.

Modern humans

About 100,000 years ago modern humans – *Homo sapiens sapiens* (us) – evolved in Africa, and began to spread around the world. They gradually replaced all other groups of people, including the Neanderthals.

Neanderthal people probably performed ceremonies for their dead.

Homo sapiens were the first humans to use paintings and carvings to communicate.

For thousands of years our ancestors got their food from wild plants and animals. They moved from place to place with the seasons. Then, around 10,000 years ago, people in different parts of the world started to farm. They planted crops and began to tame and keep animals. Many now settled in villages, where they lived throughout the year. Over time such settlements grew into complex societies.

So what is a human?

One small but significant thing that makes humans different from apes is our long thumb. All primates have 'opposable thumbs' – thumbs that can bend across the palm – but the human thumb is especially long. This makes it possible for us to carry out delicate tasks. Another advantage that we have over our ape cousins is our large brain. We are probably the most intelligent animal that has ever lived on Earth. This has allowed us to make tools, to create cultures, and to develop language.

Our ideas and memories do not die with us, but survive in forms such as painting, books and film. We have made huge changes to the Earth's environment. We have built our homes in every part of the world from the frozen Arctic Circle to the hottest desert.

▲ These rock engravings in Algeria are 7000 years old. Paintings done by early humans have been found from as far back as 40,000 years ago.

 key words

- cells
- early ancestors
- tools

In prehistoric times, people lived to an average age of only 18 years. Romans in AD 600 lived to about age 30, on average. In the year 2000, people in the developed world could expect to live to an average age of over 70.

Building bodies

A human body is made of millions of tiny building blocks called cells. A cell is the basic unit of all living things. We have about 50 million million cells in our body. Most cells are so small that it would take 100,000 to cover a pinhead. All cells have the same basic contents, but their shapes vary according to their jobs. Nerve cells are long and thin so that they can carry electrical messages to and from the brain.

▶ A close-up of heart-muscle tissues. You can see the individual cells. Every cell has a nucleus, which contains the genetic material – the instructions for making a complete human being.

▼ The different systems of the human body.

More cells

When we grow, we produce more cells. If we are injured and cells are damaged, they must be replaced. Most cells reproduce by dividing in two. Some, such as those in the intestine, are easily worn away and live for only a few days. Others, such as blood cells live for a few months and bone cells can last for 30 years.

Nervous system
The brain, spinal cord and the network of nerves are the body's communication system.

Respiratory system
The nose, windpipe and lungs work together to extract the oxygen we need from air.

Circulatory system
The heart and blood are the body's distribution and transport network.

Excretory system
The kidneys and bladder filter the blood and remove waste.

Digestive system
Breaks down our food so that we can absorb the nutrients we need.

Bones and muscles
These keep us upright and make it possible for us to move.

Reproductive system
The reproductive systems of men and women work together to produce new humans.

Tissues and organs

Few cells work alone in the body. Groups of similar cells fit together and work as units called tissues; for example, muscle cells form muscle tissue. The body's organs are made up of several different kinds of tissue. The heart, for example, is built up of muscle, nerve and connective tissues. Groups of organs that work together make up the systems of our body, such as the nervous system and the digestive system.

PERFECT PROTECTION

Soft and stretchy, but strong and protective, skin covers your entire body. It is a flexible coating that can repair itself. Extra protection comes from a natural sun-blocker made by the skin, and from our fingernails.

Skin is only a few millimetres thick, but it is an effective barrier against the outside world. Skin is waterproof, and as long as it is not cut or scratched it can keep out germs. Cells near the surface divide all the time, producing new cells to heal small wounds and replace skin that wears away.

Nails and hair

Both nails and hair grow from roots in the skin. They are made of dead cells hardened with a substance called keratin.

Our prehistoric ancestors had thick, long hair all over the body, which kept them warm. Today we have long hair only on our

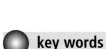

key words

- hair
- nails
- sweat
- touch

▼ A cross-section through the skin. The skin has two main layers: a thin epidermis on the surface, and a thicker dermis below.

▲ Ultraviolet rays from sunlight can do permanent damage to skin. To keep them out, the skin produces a dark pigment called melanin. More melanin means a deeper skin colour, and better protection.

Every one of the 6 billion people in the world has a different fingerprint – the swirling pattern of ridges on our fingertips.

head. The rest of the body has short, sparse hairs. Each hair has its own tiny muscle to lift it when we are cold.

Temperature control

Whether the outside temperature is hot or cold, the temperature inside our bodies stays at 37 °C. Skin helps us to keep to this constant temperature. Around 3 million sweat glands in the skin produce cooling sweat when things get too hot. And in cold weather, tiny blood vessels threaded through the skin shut down, to prevent the warm blood from being cooled.

A delicate touch

Thousands of different sensors just below the skin surface give us our delicate sense of touch. Some tell us if our surroundings are hot or cold; others respond to pain, the light touch of a feather or the pressure of a new shoe. Our lips and fingertips are the most sensitive parts of the body.

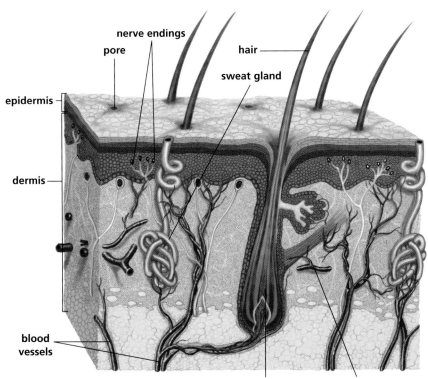

nerve endings
pore
hair
sweat gland
epidermis
dermis
blood vessels
hair follicle
oil gland

THE BARE BONES

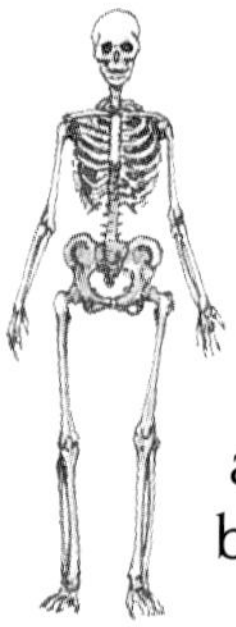

Your skeleton is a scaffolding of more than 200 living bones. It supports you and keeps you upright. The skeleton may seem fragile, but it carries the whole weight of the body. Your muscles are attached to this bony scaffolding. They pull on the bones to make you move.

The word skeleton comes from a Greek word meaning dried up, but bones are not dry or brittle. Bones are alive. They grow as we do, repair themselves if they are broken and become stronger as we exercise. A living bone has layers of hard calcium phosphate on the outside, and a honeycomb of hard bone and living cells within. This makes it strong and light.

Bony protection

Most organs of the body are soft and delicate. Our bones protect these soft organs from injury. The skull bones, for example, fit tightly together to form a tough case for the brain. The ribs form a rigid cage around the lungs and heart, and the hip bones enclose the bladder and intestines.

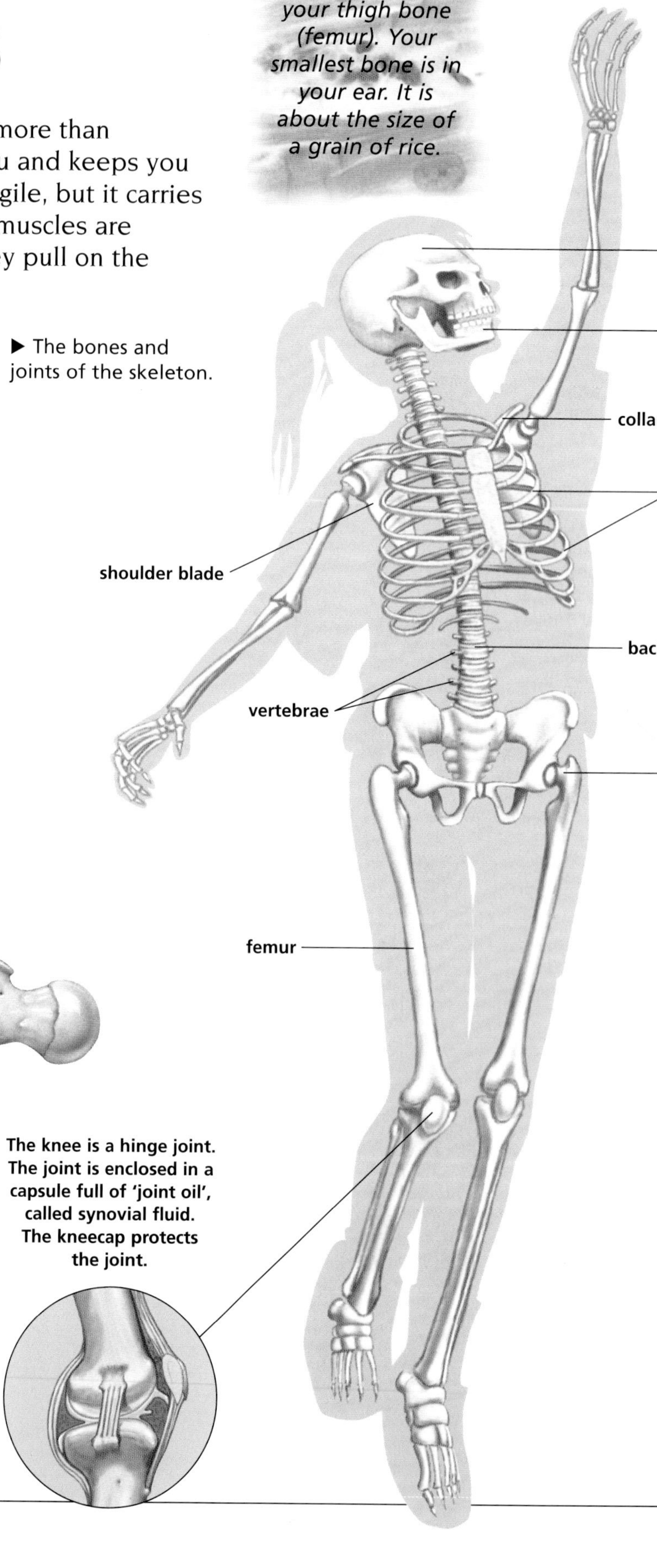

▶ The bones and joints of the skeleton.

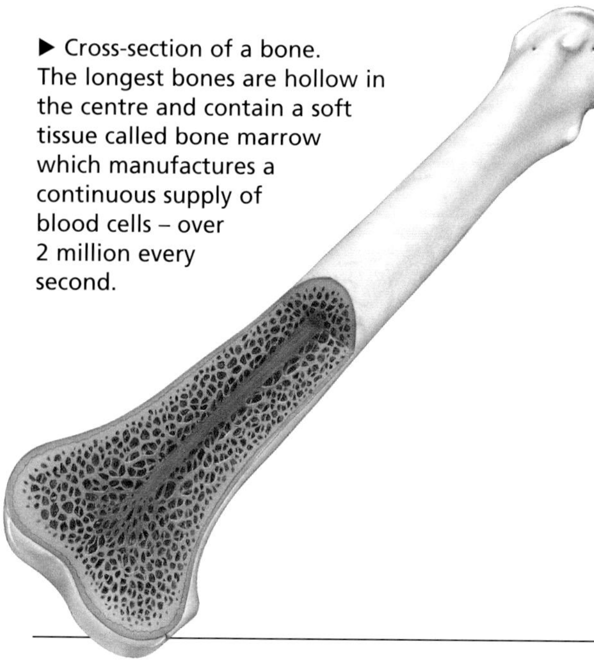

The longest bone in your body is your thigh bone (femur). Your smallest bone is in your ear. It is about the size of a grain of rice.

- skull
- jaw
- collar bone
- ribs
- shoulder blade
- backbone
- vertebrae
- hip
- femur

▶ Cross-section of a bone. The longest bones are hollow in the centre and contain a soft tissue called bone marrow which manufactures a continuous supply of blood cells – over 2 million every second.

The knee is a hinge joint. The joint is enclosed in a capsule full of 'joint oil', called synovial fluid. The kneecap protects the joint.

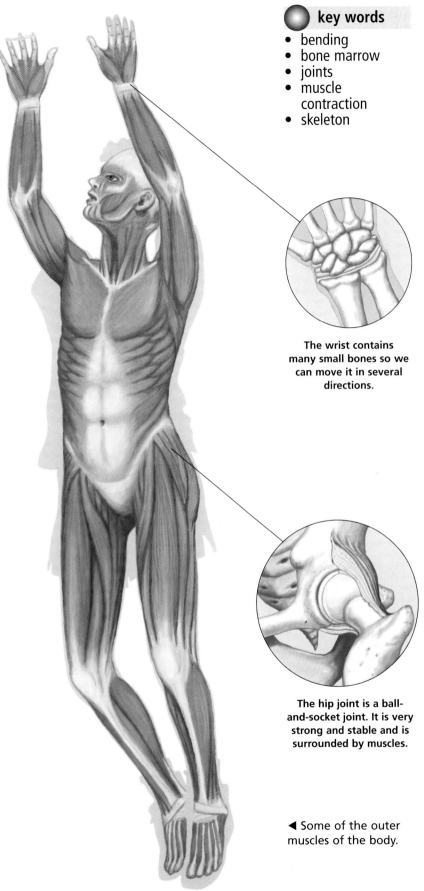

◄ Some of the outer muscles of the body.

key words

- bending
- bone marrow
- joints
- muscle contraction
- skeleton

The wrist contains many small bones so we can move it in several directions.

The hip joint is a ball-and-socket joint. It is very strong and stable and is surrounded by muscles.

Joints

Bones join each other at joints. We have different types of joint for moving in different ways. Hinge joints at the knee and elbow allow our limbs to bend like the hinge on a door. Ball-and-socket joints at the shoulder and hip allow movement in almost any direction. Each individual joint in the spine allows only a little movement, but together the 20 or so joints in our back allow us to twist and bend with ease.

Muscles and movement

Muscles account for about 40 per cent of the body's weight. We have about 600 muscles that we can control at will. These are our skeletal muscles. But we have other muscles that work automatically, such as the heart muscles, muscles in the digestive system and muscles involved in breathing.

Muscles are usually attached to two bones across a joint. Within every muscle are thousands of long, thin muscle fibres, collected together in bundles. Nerve connections from the brain run through the bundles of muscle fibres. The fibres contract (shorten) when they get a signal from the nerves to do so.

▼ Muscles can only move us by contracting. Contraction is a pulling force. Because an individual muscle can only pull, muscles usually work in pairs. One muscle contracts to move a joint in one direction. Its partner contracts to move the joint back again. In the upper arm, the biceps muscle contracts to bend the arm, while the triceps contracts to straighten it.

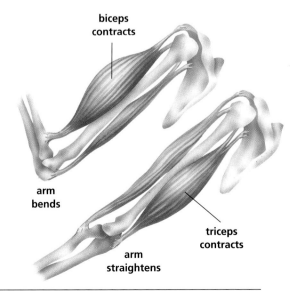

biceps contracts

arm bends

triceps contracts

arm straightens

FOOD FOR LIFE

fatty foods simple sugars and 'junk food' keep to a minimum – or an occasional treat

protein foods eat a little of these foods with meals

fruit and vegetables eat at every meal and include as snacks

carbohydrate-rich foods eat at every meal and include as snacks

▲ This food pyramid can be used as a guide to healthy eating.

Some people say, 'you are what you eat'. And it's true – our bodies are made from the food we eat. Food contains all the nutrients – the raw materials – our bodies need to build everything from muscles and bones to the brain and the heart.

Food is broken down in our digestive system into its basic parts. These parts are then put together again inside the body to make us what we are. Food also provides the energy to keep us alive.

There are three main kinds of nutrient in food – carbohydrates, proteins and fats. We also need small amounts of other nutrients called vitamins and minerals.

Food for energy and growing

Carbohydrates should make up the bulk of what we eat. They are sugary and starchy foods that give us energy for everything we do. The more active we are, the more energy-giving food we need. Someone doing physical work all day will need more carbohydrates than an office worker.

There is protein in many foods, including meat, fish, cheese and beans.

Protein is essential for growth and repair of the body. Children who are growing need more protein than adults who have reached their full size.

Fats provide energy and help to insulate the body. Our bodies use fat as an energy store, and every cell needs a little fat to build its structure. The most important sources of fat are vegetable oils, animal fat, eggs and milk products. Too much fat in the diet can be bad for us. It can clog up blood vessels and make it harder for the heart to pump blood round the body.

Vitamins and minerals

We need small amounts of vitamins and minerals in our diet each day. They keep our bodies working properly and help to protect us from illness. Fruits and vegetables are rich in vitamins such as vitamin C, which is found in oranges, and vitamin A, found in carrots. Milk contains

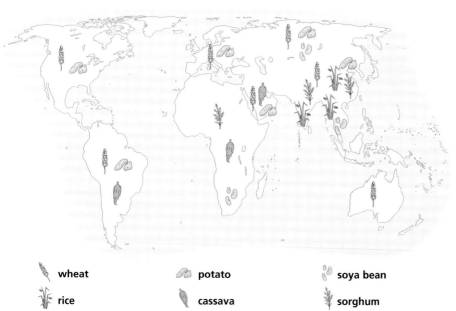

◄ Staple foods are rich in starch for energy. Wheat, barley, rye and potatoes are part of the staple diet in cooler parts of the world. Millet, rice sorghum, soya and cassava are staples in Africa and Asia.

wheat	potato	soya bean
rice	cassava	sorghum

minerals such as calcium, which we need for healthy bones, while the iron we need to make blood cells comes from meat in our diet.

Getting the balance right

To stay healthy and fit, we need to eat a variety of foods with the right mixture of carbohydrates, fats and proteins, plus some vitamins and minerals. This is what is called a balanced diet.

In most European countries and in the USA, nearly everyone has enough to eat – and some people eat too much. An average adult needs about 20 kilojoules of energy per hour for normal activities (energy is measured in kilojoules, or in calories). This is approximately a small glass of milk. During vigorous exercise this energy need goes up to 200 kilojoules. So people who do little exercise need much less food than people who are very active.

If we eat too many energy-rich foods, the excess is put into storage as fat. People who regularly eat more than they need put on weight.

In poorer countries some people are starving – they simply do not have enough to eat. Others are malnourished, because they do not get enough of the right foods.

A little of what you fancy

Most foods contain a mixture of different nutrients. For example, bread contains carbohydrate, protein, fat, vitamins, minerals and water. What people eat varies depending upon where they live. The climate affects what foods grow best. Local customs and religious beliefs are also important.

◀ Much of our food is produced in large amounts in factories. Workers wear protective clothing to keep everything clean and hygienic.

▲ This colourful market has a wide range of fruit and vegetables on sale. Fresh produce contains the highest amounts of vitamins.

Most people eat far more protein than they need. An average-sized adult needs only about 56 g per day – about half a hamburger.

● key words

- balanced diet
- carbohydrate
- fat
- protein
- staple foods

DIGESTING FOOD

Take a bite, chew and swallow, and you are starting your food on a 9-metre journey through your digestive system. The journey may take more than a day. In that time, your body will take the goodness you need from the food, and get rid of the waste.

Food helps the body to work, grow and repair itself. It contains the nutrients we need for good health. But before food is of any use, it has to be digested, or broken down into smaller parts. These can then be absorbed into the blood and used anywhere in the body.

The digestive system is a long, winding tube running right through the body. We put food into it at one end (the mouth), and waste material leaves through an opening called the anus at the other end.

Journey to the stomach

Digestion begins in the mouth as teeth tear and grind our food into tiny pieces. As we chew, the pieces mix with a watery liquid called saliva, which makes them slippery

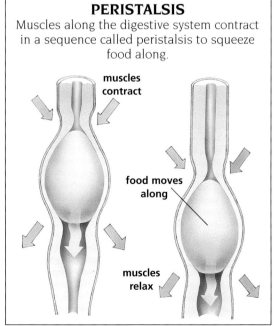

PERISTALSIS
Muscles along the digestive system contract in a sequence called peristalsis to squeeze food along.

muscles contract

food moves along

muscles relax

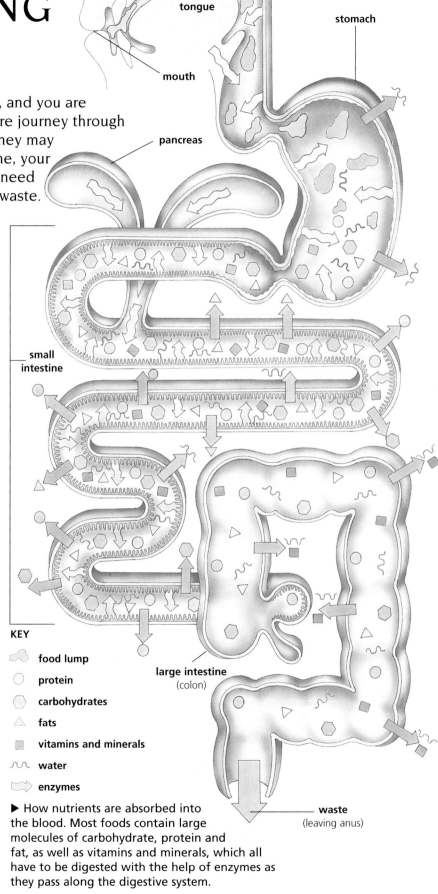

tongue

mouth

pancreas

small intestine

stomach

large intestine
(colon)

waste
(leaving anus)

KEY

- 〰 **food lump**
- ○ **protein**
- ⬡ **carbohydrates**
- △ **fats**
- ▪ **vitamins and minerals**
- ∿∿ **water**
- ⇨ **enzymes**

▶ How nutrients are absorbed into the blood. Most foods contain large molecules of carbohydrate, protein and fat, as well as vitamins and minerals, which all have to be digested with the help of enzymes as they pass along the digestive system.

TEETH

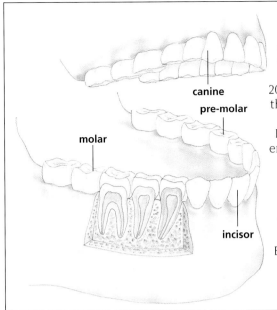

A full set of adult teeth is 32. There are eight flat incisors at the front for cutting up food, four pointed canine teeth at the side for tearing, and 20 flat-topped pre-molars and molars at the back of the mouth, for grinding and crushing food.

Every tooth is covered by tough white enamel, which protects the softer bone-like dentine beneath. Enamel is the hardest substance in the body and resists almost everything, except the acid produced by certain bacteria. These bacteria feed on bits of sugary food left on the teeth.

Brushing teeth helps to get rid of food particles and bacteria. Fluoride toothpaste actually strengthens the enamel, too.

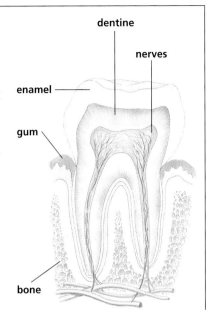

and easier to swallow. As we swallow, muscles squeeze little balls of food down the food pipe (the oesophagus) to the stomach, where they will stay for about three hours. The stomach turns the food over and over, and mixes it with digestive juices that pour from the stomach walls. Strong acid in these juices kills any bacteria you may have eaten. Eventually, all the food turns into a soupy liquid.

Little by little, the liquid trickles out of the stomach into the small intestine. Here, glands in the pancreas add more digestive juices, which complete the digestion process.

 key words

- absorption
- digestive juices
- enamel
- teeth
- villi

▼ This is an enlarged photograph of villi. These tiny folds in the lining of the small intestine give a huge area for absorbing food.

The cells which line the digestive system are rapidly worn away by the food which flows past them. Cells have to be replaced every 2–3 days.

Absorbing activities

Once food has been digested, the nutrients from it can be absorbed into the blood. This happens in a long section of the intestine called the the ileum. Uncoiled, the ileum is 5–6 metres long, more than three times the height of a person. Its thin, creased lining is made of millions of tiny folds called villi. Villi increase the total area available for absorbing food to around 10 square metres, about the area of a small room. Each of the villi contains tiny blood vessels called capillaries, which collect nutrients and carry them quickly away.

Waste disposal

Not everything we eat can be digested. Undigested food passes from the ileum into the large intestine, or colon. Here, the body reabsorbs most of the liquid that was added to the food during the digestive process. The soft lumps of waste (the faeces) pass into the rectum, where they are stored. Eventually they leave the body through the anus.

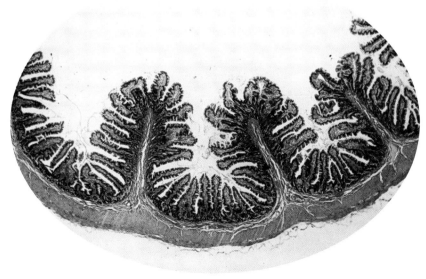

CHEMICAL CONTROL

The liver is the body's chemical factory. It is the largest organ in the body, and one of the busiest – it carries out more than 500 different tasks. One of its main jobs is to process the nutrients we absorb from our food.

The liver has many different roles. It produces a substance called bile, one of the digestive juices. It recognizes many harmful drugs and poisons, and renders them harmless before they can do any damage. And it recycles old red blood cells.

Import control

Four-fifths of the blood going to the liver comes directly from the digestive system. The liver removes some nutrients from the blood, passing on only those we need for our daily needs. If we have too much glucose from sugary or starchy foods, the liver will take up sugar from the blood and store it. These stores can be quickly released if sugar levels get low.

The liver also absorbs and stores fat and some vitamins. It uses one of these vitamins, vitamin B12, for making new red blood cells. The liver also recycles old red blood cells. Some of the chemicals

▼ Jaundice is a yellowness of the skin, which is caused by diseases of the liver or gall bladder.

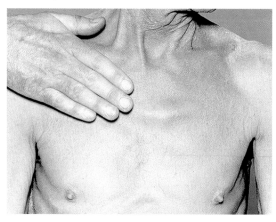

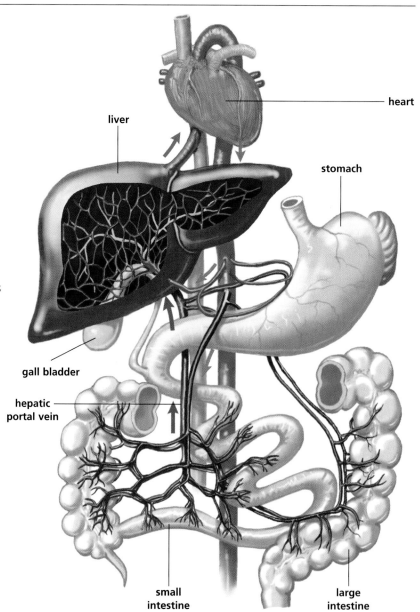

▲ Blood from the digestive system arrives at the liver in the hepatic portal vein. Once the liver has processed the blood, it passes into the main blood system. Bile from the liver is stored in a small sac called the gall bladder.

from these old cells are used to make the bile, which is stored in the gall bladder.

Some nutrients that the liver receives cannot be stored at all. If there is too much protein or vitamin C, for example, the liver must remove them altogether. It converts excess proteins into urea, which is sent to the kidneys and leaves the body in urine.

By the time blood leaves the liver, it has the correct balance of nutrients for all the body's needs.

key words
- bile
- disposal
- storage

BALANCING WATER

Nearly two-thirds of your body is water. You gain water as you eat and drink. But you lose about a litre and a half each day through sweating, breathing and in the urine. Our kidneys have the delicate task of keeping the balance between water coming in and water going out exactly right.

The amount of water our bodies lose or gain depends on the outside temperature and on what we are doing. If it is hot we sweat, and unless we drink plenty of water, we will need to conserve the water inside us. If it is cool and we have plenty to drink, we will need to get rid of water.

▼ On the right of this photograph you can see a large, branched kidney stone. Kidney stones can block the flow of urine from the kidneys.

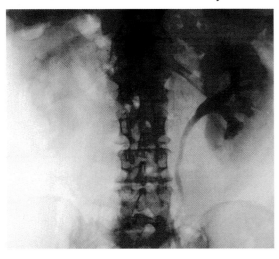

Filtering the blood

As well as balancing the water in our bodies, the kidneys filter and clean out the blood. Each kidney is made up of millions of tiny filtering units called nephrons. The nephrons can filter about 4 litres of blood every 5 minutes. Each day about 200 litres of water leaves the blood and passes into the filters. Most of it is then reclaimed and returns to the blood. Only about a litre per day stays in the nephrons, to leave the kidney and flow into the bladder as urine.

key words
- filter
- urea
- urine

Waste disposal

As well as water, urine contains unwanted salts and urea, a waste substance made by the liver. Urea is poisonous, so the kidneys remove all of it from the blood.

The liquid which leaves the kidneys as urine is about 96 per cent water and just 4 per cent salts and urea. Urine runs down two tubes called the ureters from the kidneys into the bladder. This is a stretchable bag where the urine can be stored. The bladder can hold about half a litre before we must empty it.

▶ The kidneys are just under the ribs in your back. Below and between them is the bladder. The kidneys contain millions of long, U-shaped tubules called nephrons. Capillaries which surround each nephron reabsorb all the useful materials and most of the water. Unwanted substances pass to the very end of the nephron.

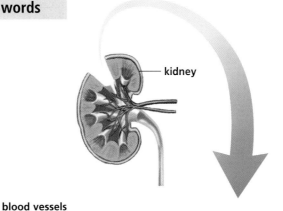

kidney

blood vessels (capillaries)

nephrons

nutrients and water reabsorbed into blood

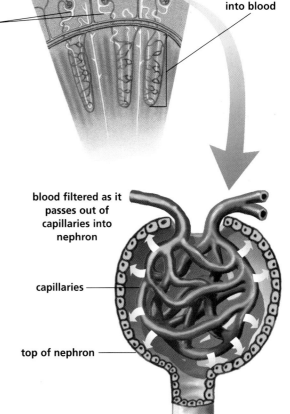

blood filtered as it passes out of capillaries into nephron

capillaries

top of nephron

EVERY BREATH YOU TAKE

From the day we are born to the day we die, we breathe every few seconds. We may take as many as 20,000 breaths a day. We breathe air because we need a constant supply of the oxygen it contains to fuel our activities. Our lungs extract the oxygen, and send it via the blood to all our cells.

Your body needs energy to power the activities of every cell. Energy comes from the food you eat. It is released during respiration, a chemical process that takes place in every cell. Respiration uses oxygen and produces carbon dioxide as a waste product. Breathing in draws in the oxygen, and breathing out gets rid of the waste carbon dioxide.

key words

- alveoli
- cilia
- inhalation
- oxygen
- windpipe

In and out

Your nose, windpipe, lungs and chest muscles make up your breathing system. Lungs have no muscles of their own, so the muscles of the chest do the work of breathing.

▼ As we breathe in, the diaphragm is lowered and the ribs move up and out to draw air into the lungs.

LUNG DISEASES

People who live in places where the air is polluted, or who smoke, are more likely to suffer from lung diseases. Bronchitis is a disease in which the linings of the air passages (bronchi) become inflamed. In asthma, the muscles in the bronchi contract, and restrict the flow of air. One form of asthma treatment is to use an inhaler containing a drug that relaxes the muscles of the bronchi.

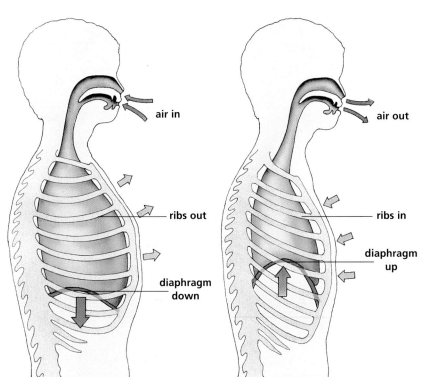

air in

ribs out

diaphragm down

air out

ribs in

diaphragm up

Most important of all is the diaphragm, a flat sheet of muscle covering the floor of the chest. As the diaphragm pushes downwards, it reduces pressure on the lungs and creates more space inside your chest. Air rushes in to fill the lungs. During gentle breathing, the diaphragm moves only a centimetre or two. As you exercise, it may move 6 or 7 centimetres. When you take a really deep breath, muscles between the ribs lift them upwards to make even more space in your chest.

Breathing out is the reverse of breathing in. Muscles lower the ribs, and the diaphragm arches upwards. The lungs are squeezed, and air and carbon dioxide are forced out.

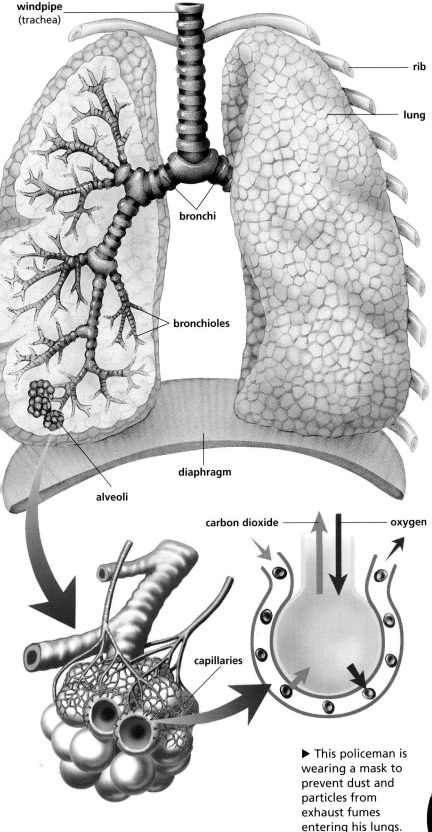

windpipe
(trachea)

rib

lung

bronchi

bronchioles

diaphragm

alveoli

carbon dioxide ——— oxygen

capillaries

▲ Oxygen is exchanged for waste carbon dioxide through the thin walls of the alveoli. Alveoli are arranged in groups which resemble bunches of grapes.

◀ Air enters the lungs through the nose and mouth, and passes down the windpipe. The windpipe divides into two bronchi, which in turn divide into bronchioles and finally into alveoli. Each of your lungs has over 200 million alveoli.

After vigorous exercise you may breathe up to 10 times faster than when you are resting, to get all the oxygen your body needs.

Inside the lungs

Air travels to the lungs through the nostrils and down the windpipe, or trachea. Inside the lungs it passes into smaller and smaller branching passageways. Each tiny passageway ends in a group of air sacs called alveoli. Hundreds of millions of aveoli make up the lungs. It has been estimated that if they were flat, they would cover a tennis court. An adult's lungs hold about 5 litres of air.

The walls of the alveoli are thinner than tissue paper, and are covered with tiny blood vessels, or capillaries. Oxygen easily seeps through these capillaries into the blood, while carbon dioxide from the blood goes in the other direction.

Keeping the lungs clean

The air around us is often dirty, and dirt and dust can harm the alveoli. So the air is cleaned on the way to the lungs. Hairs in the nose catch the largest particles. Smaller particles are trapped in the windpipe, and air passages by a sticky liquid called mucus. The mucus passes up to the throat and is swallowed or sneezed or blown out.

▶ This policeman is wearing a mask to prevent dust and particles from exhaust fumes entering his lungs.

OUR TRANSPORT SYSTEM

A city needs a transport system to carry people and goods from place to place. In the same way our bodies need a transport system to carry nutrients and oxygen. The body's method of transport is the blood. Blood flows to every part of the body, travelling through a complex network of tubes.

The network that carries our blood is made up of tubes, or vessels, called arteries, veins and capillaries. Blood is pumped around this network by the heart. Arteries are the largest and strongest vessels. They divide into smaller and smaller vessels. The smallest ones are called capillaries.

Collection and delivery

Capillaries are so small that they can fit between cells. Their walls are so thin that food and oxygen from the blood can pass straight through into the cells. Waste from the cells passes back into the blood to be carried

▶ The heart has four chambers. The upper chambers, the atria, pump blood to the ventricles. The lower chambers, the ventricles, are larger and pump blood out of the heart. The left ventricle pumps blood all round the body.

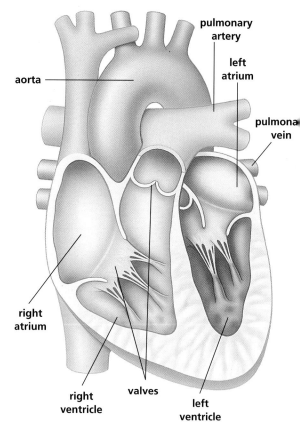

aorta

pulmonary artery

left atrium

pulmonary vein

right atrium

right ventricle

valves

left ventricle

away. The capillaries join up again, making larger tubes, which in turn join to become veins. Blood travels more slowly as it makes its way back to the heart. Larger veins have valves inside them to keep blood moving in the right direction.

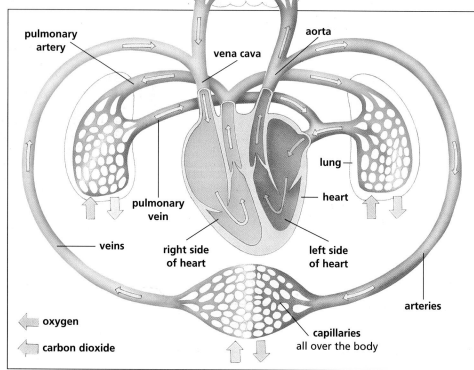

brain

pulmonary artery

vena cava

aorta

lung

pulmonary vein

heart

veins

right side of heart

left side of heart

arteries

oxygen

carbon dioxide

capillaries all over the body

THE HEART

Your heart is made up of two separate pumps. The right-hand pump receives blood from the body and sends it to the lungs through the pulmonary arteries. In the lungs, the blood picks up oxygen. Then it returns to the left side of the heart through the pulmonary veins.

The left side of the heart then pumps this oxygenated blood through arteries to organs and muscles all over the body. Through capillaries in the organs and muscles, the blood gives up its oxygen and collects waste carbon dioxide.

When it has done this, the blood returns in veins to the right side of the heart, to be sent to the lungs for more oxygen.

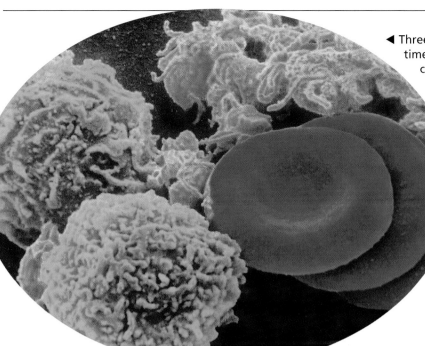

◀ Three different types of blood cell magnified many times. In this picture, the white blood cells are coloured blue. The cells coloured pink are platelets. Platelets help to seal cuts in the skin. They clump together to form clots and produce a mass of fibres (shown here in orange) that trap red blood cells and dry to form a scab.

What is blood?

Almost half of the blood in your body is made up of red blood cells. These tiny red discs contain a substance called haemoglobin. This picks up oxygen in the lungs and releases it into the cells, which need it for energy.

Blood also contains a smaller number of white blood cells – about one for every 500 red cells. Their job is to fight infections. All the blood cells are swept along in a liquid called plasma, which contains dissolved chemicals and carbon dioxide. Fresh supplies of blood cells are continually made in the bone marrow.

The pump that never tires

The driving force that keeps your blood moving is your heart. The heart is made of a special type of muscle called cardiac muscle, which never gets tired. Day and night, every beat is a muscle contraction that forces about 60 millilitres of blood on its way. The heart of an adult at rest beats about 70 times a minute, but this can double during exercise.

Like any active muscle, the heart needs a good supply of blood. Sometimes the blood vessels to the heart become narrow or blocked. This causes a heart attack. Smokers and people who are overweight have a higher risk of heart attacks than others.

key words

- artery
- blood
- clotting
- heart attack
- pump

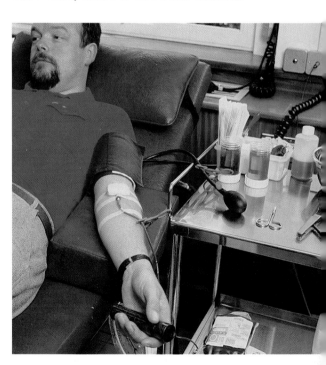

▶ A blood donor gives about 500ml of blood, which can be stored for a few weeks. The blood can be given to another person of the same blood group.

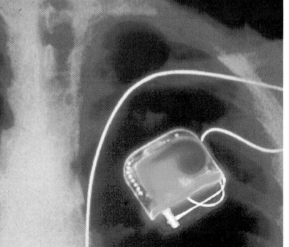

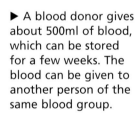

◀ Sometimes the heart's natural pacemaker, which controls heart rate, fails because of heart disease. The person in this X-ray has had an artificial pacemaker implanted in their chest, which allows them to lead a normal, active life

Your heart beats non-stop, 24 hours a day, 7 days a week. If you live to be 70, that comes to over 2.5 billion heartbeats!

CHEMICAL MESSENGERS

Imagine being woken at night by a strange noise, or being chased by a vicious dog. Your heart starts thumping, you breathe more quickly and you break out in a sweat. All these changes are caused by a chemical messenger called adrenaline, which prepares you to react to danger.

Adrenaline is just one of many chemical messengers that your body produces. We call these messengers hormones. Some, like adrenaline, affect many parts of the body. Others may affect only one organ.

There are thousands of different processes going on in your body at any one moment. Hormones help to control these processes. They make sure that you grow at a steady rate, and that you always have the right amount of sugar in your blood. Hormones also control the changes that happen at puberty, when you become sexually mature, and during pregnancy.

▲ This boy has goitre – a swollen thyroid gland in his neck. It may be caused by a lack of iodine in his diet or because the gland itself is not working properly.

Blood messengers

Hormones are made in glands known as endocrine glands, which pour them straight into the blood. Hormones are not released all the time – they are produced in short bursts. And cells respond to hormones at different speeds. This means that hormones can control anything from slow processes such as growing up to the high-speed reaction to an emergency.

▼ How the hormone insulin works. Insulin is produced in the pancreas. It acts on the liver and muscles to stop the level of glucose in the blood from getting too high.

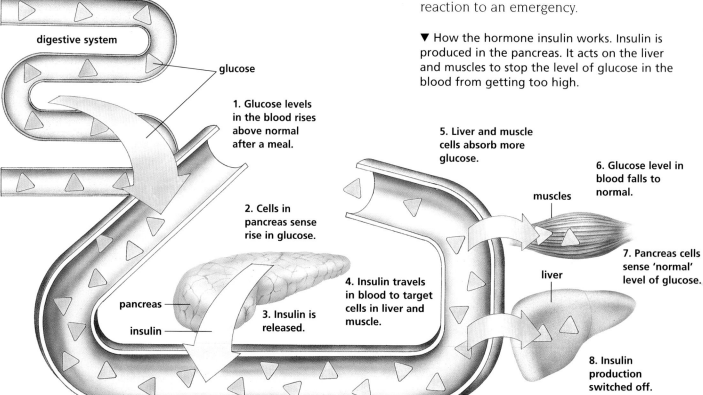

digestive system

glucose

1. Glucose levels in the blood rises above normal after a meal.

2. Cells in pancreas sense rise in glucose.

pancreas

insulin

3. Insulin is released.

4. Insulin travels in blood to target cells in liver and muscle.

5. Liver and muscle cells absorb more glucose.

6. Glucose level in blood falls to normal.

muscles

liver

7. Pancreas cells sense 'normal' level of glucose.

8. Insulin production switched off.

pituitary

thyroid

THE BODY'S HORMONES

Pituitary: controls activity of thyroid, adrenal and reproductive glands. Other hormones stimulate the womb to contract during birth, and stimulate milk production after a baby is born.

Thyroid: thyroxine controls the rate at which we grow, and how fast food is converted to energy in our cells.

Adrenal glands: adrenaline speeds up the heart and breathing, causes sweating and diverts blood to the muscles, in response to an emergency. Cortisone helps fight stress and shock. Aldosterone helps regulate water and salt in the blood.

Pancreas: insulin controls the body's use of glucose.

Ovaries: oestrogen and progesterone control female appearance and the release of eggs, and prepare the body for pregnancy.

Testes: testosterone controls the development of male appearance and the production of sperm cells.

adrenal
glands

pancreas

ovaries
(in female only)

key words
- adrenaline
- control
- insulin
- pituitary
- thyroid

testes
(in male only)

The world's tallest woman, Sandy Allen, grew to a height of 2.22 metres because of an excess of growth hormone.

Hormone control centre

The pituitary gland, attached to the underside of the brain, releases hormones that control the activities of other endocrine glands. It also produces other hormones, for example one that controls the amount of water filtered in the kidneys. The pituitary is attached to the brain by the hypothalamus, which links together the nervous system and the hormonal system.

▶ People suffering from the disease diabetes do not produce enough insulin in their bodies. Their blood sugar levels can become dangerously high unless, like this girl, they give themselves regular injections of insulin.

THE NERVOUS SYSTEM

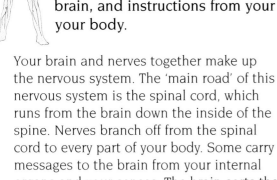

▶ Nerves connect from the brain to every part of your body. Most nerves run down the spinal cord, then branch to every part of the body.

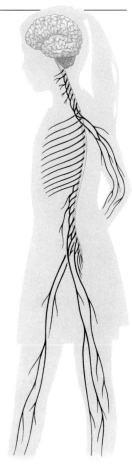

E very second, hundreds of tiny pulses of electricity shoot through your body along living wires called nerves. The electrical pulses are messengers, carrying information about the outside world to your brain, and instructions from your brain to the rest of your body.

Your brain and nerves together make up the nervous system. The 'main road' of this nervous system is the spinal cord, which runs from the brain down the inside of the spine. Nerves branch off from the spinal cord to every part of your body. Some carry messages to the brain from your internal organs and your senses. The brain sorts the information it receives and sends out messages via other nerves to control everything from your blood pressure to the way you move.

Nerve cells

Nerve cells, or neurons, can transmit electrical messages at high speed. Each neuron has several 'inputs', called dendrites, along which messages travel into the main cell. Leading out from the cell is a single 'output', the axon. This connects to another nerve, or to a muscle or other cell. Neurons do not touch one another. Messages cross the gap, or synapse, between one neuron and the next with the help of a chemical.

Outside the brain, neurons connect to each other in simple pathways. But within the brain itself, the neurons are interconnected in an amazingly complex network. Only some of these billions upon billions of interconnections are ever used. But new pathways are always opening up as we have new experiences, learn new things, and lay down new memories.

▼ Two connecting nerve cells. Dendrites bring messages into the cell, the axon sends messages out. Axons have a fatty covering which speeds up transmission.

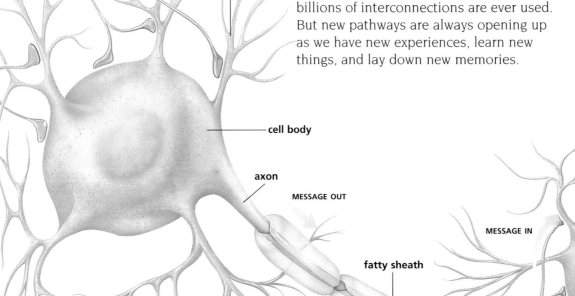

dendrites

cell body

axon

MESSAGE OUT

fatty sheath

MESSAGE IN

synapse (gap)

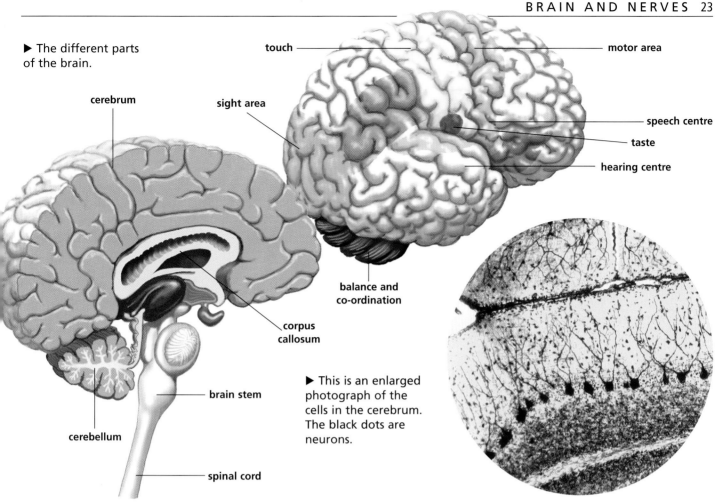

▶ The different parts of the brain.

touch

motor area

cerebrum

sight area

speech centre

taste

hearing centre

balance and co-ordination

corpus callosum

brain stem

cerebellum

spinal cord

▶ This is an enlarged photograph of the cells in the cerebrum. The black dots are neurons.

Automatic pilot

There are three important areas of the brain, each one responsible for different kinds of action. Close to the spinal cord is the brain stem. This controls automatic activities such as breathing and digestion. At the back of the brain is the cerebellum. This co-ordinates movement, conscious control and balance, allowing you to move smoothly.

The largest and most complicated part of the brain is the cerebrum. It controls your conscious actions, speech and all your senses. It also does all your thinking, and is the centre of memory and learning.

The cerebrum has two halves (cerebral hemispheres), linked by bundles of nerve fibres. Sensations from one side of the body connect to the opposite side of the brain, and movements of one side of the body are controlled by the other side of the brain. The right side is most important in artistic, creative tasks, while the left is responsible for understanding, reading and thinking.

The brain contains 100 billion neurons and there are as many again in the rest of the body.

key words
- memory
- neuron
- reflex
- spinal cord
- synapse

INSTANT ACTIONS

Sometimes we do not have time to think – in an emergency we must act right away. For example, if you tread on a sharp stone with bare feet, you immediately pull your foot away. An action like this is called a reflex.

A simple reflex is controlled by the nerves of the spinal cord without involving the brain. Messages pass from pain receptors in the foot along a neuron to the spinal cord. Here, the messages trigger off an immediate return signal activating the muscles of the leg.

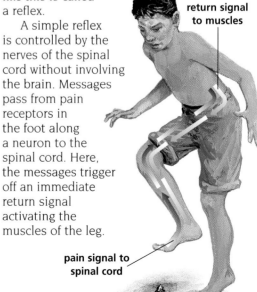

return signal to muscles

pain signal to spinal cord

SENSING THE WORLD

▶ Our most important sense organs are all located in the head.

An eagle can spot a scampering rabbit from nearly 5 kilometres away. A person would struggle to see it just 1 kilometre away. Eagles' eyes have five times more light-sensitive cells than ours. But even our eyes have more than 130 million light-sensitive cells in an area the size of a postage stamp.

Sight is our most important sense. About 80 per cent of everything we know about the world reaches us through our eyes. Our eyes and other sense organs pick up information about the outside world. They send messages to the brain, which uses the information to work out what is happening around us. Different sense organs detect different things, but they all send their messages as tiny electrical signals through a network of nerves.

nerves

outer ear

semicircular canals (organs of balance)

bones of middle ear

cochlea

The ear contains the mechanisms for hearing.

sound waves

eardrum

What can you see?

By day, the world is full of light energy, which pours from the Sun in a never-ending stream. Our eyes use this light to give us information about our surroundings. A lens at the front of the eye focuses light from outside to create a tiny picture of the world inside the eye. The inner eye is covered by a layer of light-sensitive cells called the retina. The cells send messages to the brain when light falls on them. The retina contains two types of cell – rods and cones. Rods respond to dim light, but see only shades of grey. Cones only work in bright light, but enable us to see in colour.

If you cover one eye, you will find it is hard to judge how close or far away things are. This is because each of our eyes has a slightly different view of the world. The brain uses the two views to put together a three-dimensional picture.

Hearing

The ear detects vibrations in the air, which we call sounds. Inside the ear, a series of tiny bones magnify them. In the inner chamber of the ear, called the cochlea, the vibrations send waves of movement through a fluid. The cochlea is lined with thousands of sensitive hairs. Nerve cells attached to each hair send out signals as the movement of the fluid bends the hairs. Other sensors in the ear tell us which way up we are, and help us to balance.

Scientists have recently discovered a new taste which they have called umami. It is a savoury, meaty flavour and may be the fifth taste which humans can identify.

◀ Most of the time our eyes work well, but they can be fooled. How many cubes can you see in this picture? Depending on how you look at it, you might count six or seven.

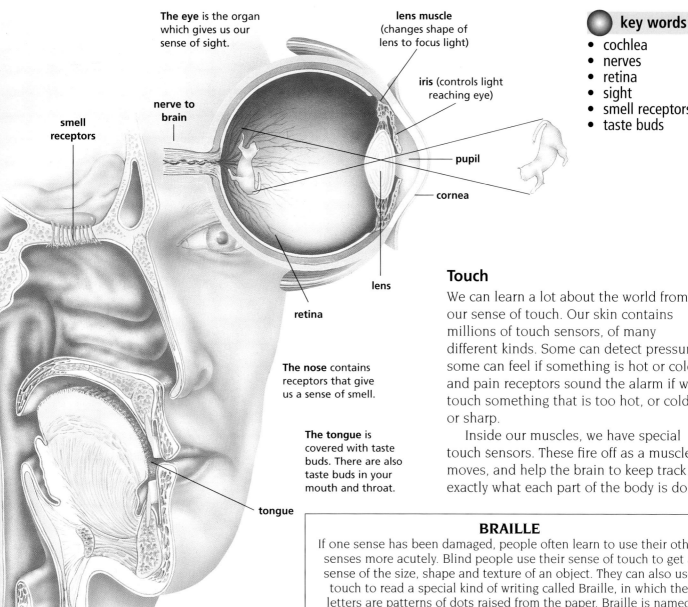

The eye is the organ which gives us our sense of sight.

lens muscle (changes shape of lens to focus light)

iris (controls light reaching eye)

smell receptors

nerve to brain

pupil

cornea

lens

retina

The nose contains receptors that give us a sense of smell.

The tongue is covered with taste buds. There are also taste buds in your mouth and throat.

tongue

Touch

We can learn a lot about the world from our sense of touch. Our skin contains millions of touch sensors, of many different kinds. Some can detect pressure, some can feel if something is hot or cold, and pain receptors sound the alarm if we touch something that is too hot, or cold, or sharp.

Inside our muscles, we have special touch sensors. These fire off as a muscle moves, and help the brain to keep track of exactly what each part of the body is doing.

BRAILLE

If one sense has been damaged, people often learn to use their other senses more acutely. Blind people use their sense of touch to get a sense of the size, shape and texture of an object. They can also use touch to read a special kind of writing called Braille, in which the letters are patterns of dots raised from the paper. Braille is named after its inventor, the Frenchman Louis Braille (1809–1852).

Taste and smell

Smell and taste receptors in our nose and tongue work closely together. We learn this from experience. When we have a blocked nose, our food does not taste as good, because we cannot smell it as well as taste it.

Both smell and taste receptors respond to chemicals. We can distinguish four different tastes – sweet, sour, bitter and salt. Bitterness receptors are the most sensitive, possibly because poisons are bitter-tasting. Our noses can identify a wide variety of different smells.

ALL IN THE MIND

Our brain is so astonishingly complex, it's not surprising that no one really knows how we think and learn. There are more than 100 billion nerve cells in the brain, each one connected to thousands of others. Communication between the cells never stops; each one can send up to 300 electrical signals every second.

We do know that as we grow and learn, new pathways are made between groups of nerve cells. The more we use a pathway, the more efficient it becomes and the more easily we can use it. This is how we learn a new skill or remember information. Your brain changes all the time as it adapts to new inputs and learns new skills.

Learning and remembering

People learn in many different ways, and learning goes on throughout our lives. We learn by trial and error: babies pick up a rattle and discover that shaking it makes a noise. As we grow up, we use the same method to find out which tin is full of biscuits and which is empty. If all our problems had to be solved by trial and error, even everyday tasks would take a long time. Learning from past experience is important. We remember which key opens a door – we do not have to try each key in the bunch every time.

We also learn by imitating others and practising what we have seen people do or heard them say. This is how we learn to speak and how we learn new languages. We can also learn about what other people have done at one remove, for instance by reading, watching television or surfing the Internet.

▲ This child will learn by trial and error as she plays with the shapes.

key words

- brainwaves
- chemicals
- emotions
- learning
- remembering

MEMORY GAME

Imagine you are going shopping and you need to remember to buy six things. Think of a story that links these things – it can be as silly as you like. The story will help you to remember the list. A story to link the items in this list might go like this:

1. You are eating **sausages** and they taste odd – they are covered with **stamps**.

2. You wash the **stamps** off the **sausages** with **shampoo**.

Shopping list
sausages
postage stamps
shampoo
chocolate
a comic
a birthday card

3. The **sausages** turn into **chocolate**. You settle down to eat the **chocolate** and read your **comic.**

4. A **birthday card** falls out of the **comic** and you remember it is your birthday.

► Emotions can be shared by large groups of people. You can see by their faces and gestures that these people are happy.

▼ Throughout the night your brain is active, sorting and storing the day's events. Brain waves show patterns of activity in different parts of the brain.

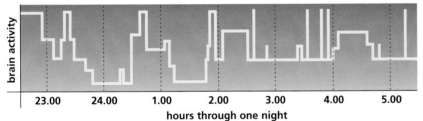

brain activity

23.00 24.00 1.00 2.00 3.00 4.00 5.00

hours through one night

Feelings and emotions

Emotions are strong feelings such as love, hate, anger and grief. These feelings begin in the brain but often they affect the whole body. When we are angry or frightened, the brain releases hormones to prepare us to take action. If we are sad or very happy, we may burst into tears.

The brain also releases other chemicals that affect the way we feel, such as endorphins and seratonin. Endorphins are sometimes called the body's own painkillers and affect the way we feel pain. Serotonin reduces anxiety and makes us feel calmer and able to cope.

Sleep

A baby sleeps for about 16 hours a day, and an adult for about eight hours. Your brain is still active when you are asleep, but in a different way. It does not register the usual messages from your senses, but it is busy dreaming. REM or rapid eye movement sleep is the period when the sleeper's eyes move as though they are watching something. Most dreaming takes place during the REM phase.

WORD OF MOUTH

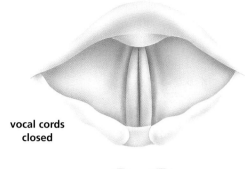

vocal cords closed

vocal cords open

Walk into your school playground any morning and you'll hear a babble of conversation. Speech is a really good way of communicating. When we speak, our vocal cords contract and relax very fast, we change the shape of our mouth, and move our tongue, lips and teeth very quickly and precisely. We learn to do all this in the first few years of life.

The speech centre in the left side of the brain controls language. The brain recognizes not only the words that are being spoken, but also identifies who is talking by the sound of their voice.

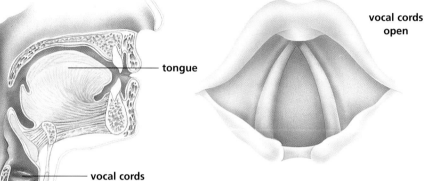

tongue

vocal cords

larynx

windpipe

◀ ▲ Our voice box or larynx is at the top of the windpipe. Our vocal chords are stretched across the larynx. Air from the lungs makes the cords vibrate, and muscles pull them tighter or relax them to change the pitch of the sound.

First words

Scientists believe that humans are born with the ability to learn language. At first babies babble, making and listening to their own sounds. As they grow older, they start to imitate what they hear and to put words together. A child's first language will be the one spoken by the people around them.

Grammar is the elaborate set of rules we use to put words together so that they make sense. Even experts are not able to explain all the rules of grammar, and yet by the age of three most children will know how to speak in reasonably correct sentences. As we grow and develop, we learn to use language to express more complex ideas.

Body language

As well as speaking with our voices, we communicate with our hands and bodies. It is quite easy to see when someone is angry, puzzled or surprised just by looking at their face. Some gestures, such as nodding or shaking the head, take the place of words.

key words

- gestures
- grammar
- larynx
- talking

▼ People who are deaf can learn to communicate entirely through gestures and signs. This person is using sign language to say 'Hello! I am pleased to meet you.'

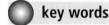

Hello!   **I**   **(am)**   **pleased**   **to meet**   **you.**

IN YOUR GENES

Can you roll your tongue? If you can, the chances are you will find someone else in your family who can do it too. One in four of us are tongue-rollers. It is just one of the thousands of characteristics that we may inherit from our parents through our genes.

Every child is like their parents in some ways, but each of us has our own unique combination of genes. Apart from identical twins, no two people have the same genes.

▲ Identical twins develop from one fertilized egg that separates into two halves. They have exactly the same genes and chromosomes, so they look almost exactly alike.

Chromosomes and genes

Your genetic material is found in the nucleus of every cell in your body. It is in the form of chromosomes, fine strands of a chemical called DNA. Each cell contains pairs of corresponding chromosomes, which carry genes for the same characteristics.

Humans have a total of 46 chromosomes – 23 pairs – in all their cells, except for the sperm and egg cells, which have 23 unpaired chromosomes. When the sperm and egg cells join, the chromosomes from the mother and father pair up, so that the new baby has its own unique set of 46 chromosomes.

Problem genes

Some combinations of genes can cause disorders and diseases, and some of these affect men more than women. For example, about 8 per cent of men are colour blind – they cannot distinguish the colours red and green. It is rare for women to be colour blind, but many women are carriers. This means that they can pass on the problem genes to their children.

The human genome project is an international research programme to work out the sequence of all the genes on our chromosomes. Now the whole sequence has been worked out, finding faulty genes will become much easier, and new treatments for genetic diseases may result.

key words
- chromosomes
- DNA
- genes

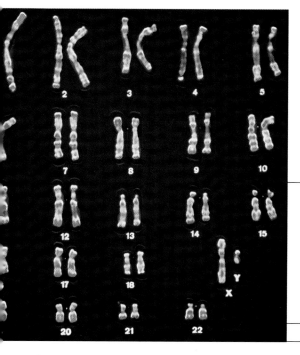

CHROMOSOMES
The 23 pairs of human chromosomes. One half of each pair comes from the mother and the other half from the father. Bottom right are the sex chromosomes. This person has an X chromosome and a Y chromosome, and so is male. Every egg contains an X chromosome. Sperm may contain either an X or a Y chromosome. If a sperm carrying an X chromosome joins with the egg, the child will be a girl. If a sperm carrying a Y chromosome joins with the egg, the child will be a boy.

A NEW LIFE BEGINS

At the moment of birth, a new baby emerges from its mother's body to begin a life of its own. But the baby's life really began nine months earlier, when a sperm cell fertilized an egg. Over the months that followed, the egg divided, grew and developed from a single cell to become a new human being.

Sperm cells are released into a woman's body during sexual intercourse. They then set off on a journey, swimming through the woman's womb, into the fallopian tubes that lead to the ovaries, in search of an egg. Of the 300 million or so sperm that set off, only a few hundred reach the egg. If one of these sperm succeeds in fertilizing the egg, the woman becomes pregnant.

The developing baby

Once an egg has been fertilized, it begins to grow and develop. In just a week it will become a ball of over 100 cells. At first the cells are all alike, but soon they change to form the muscles, bones, blood, heart, eyes and ears of the baby.

After eight weeks the baby is less than three centimetres long, but it has all its important organs in place. The baby continues to grow for the next seven months. It floats gently in a bag of fluid, which protects it from bumps and jolts, and it receives nourishment from its mother via the umbilical cord.

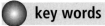

● **key words**

- birth
- egg
- fertilization
- sperm
- womb

▲ A sperm fertilizes an egg. Even though it is much smaller than the egg, it will penetrate the outer layers and fuse with the egg cell underneath.

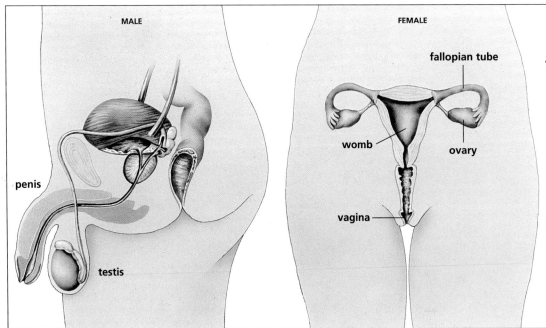

MALE

FEMALE

penis

testis

fallopian tube

womb

ovary

vagina

HUMAN SEX ORGANS

The human sex organs. The man produces sperm cells in his testes. The woman produces eggs in her ovaries, which release one egg each month. During sexual intercourse, the man's penis becomes erect, and he puts it into the woman's vagina. He releases sperm from his penis into her vagina. From here the sperm swim towards the egg. If one of them succeeds in joining with the egg, the woman becomes pregnant.

Birth

After nine months, the baby's development is complete. Birth begins when the mother's hormones stimulate the neck of the womb to open. More hormones urge the muscles of the womb to contract, gradually pushing the baby down the vagina.

Powerful contractions push the baby out of the mother's body, into the outside world. Most babies are born headfirst and take their first breath almost immediately. A newborn baby is dependent on its parents or carers for milk, warmth and protection for many months after it is born.

During its development a baby is protected inside its mother's body. As its muscles develop, she can feel the baby moving inside her. When nine months have passed the baby fills the space and cannot move very much.

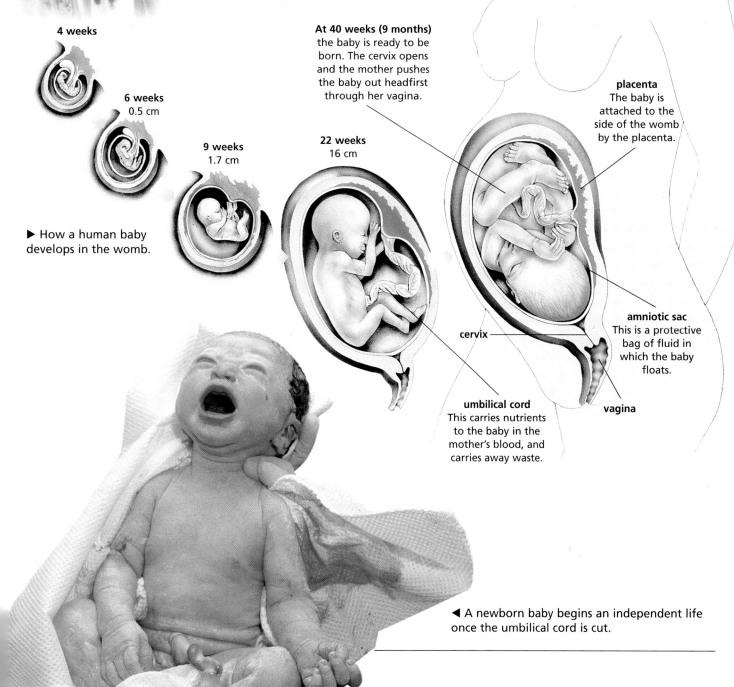

4 weeks

6 weeks
0.5 cm

9 weeks
1.7 cm

22 weeks
16 cm

At 40 weeks (9 months) the baby is ready to be born. The cervix opens and the mother pushes the baby out headfirst through her vagina.

placenta
The baby is attached to the side of the womb by the placenta.

▶ How a human baby develops in the womb.

cervix

amniotic sac
This is a protective bag of fluid in which the baby floats.

umbilical cord
This carries nutrients to the baby in the mother's blood, and carries away waste.

vagina

◀ A newborn baby begins an independent life once the umbilical cord is cut.

GROWING UP

Young babies are almost helpless: they can suck, swallow and grasp, but they must have almost everything done for them. And yet, within one or two years, they will probably be walking and starting to talk. By the age of 5 they will be able to speak fluently, draw and may be starting to read.

As babies grow to become children, and then adults, the shape and proportions of their bodies change. A baby's head makes up a quarter of its body length, but in an adult, the head accounts for only an eighth of the total height. Our bodies and minds develop much more quickly when we are babies than at any other time. Over our first few months of life, our muscles become stronger and we learn to co-ordinate our actions. New, exciting activities such as climbing the stairs, jumping and riding a bike become possible.

Growing and changing

From the age of about 5 years, a child's body grows steadily. Then, from the age of 10 years for girls and a little older for boys, there is a sudden growth spurt.

At this time, known as puberty, the ovaries of a girl start to release the sex hormone oestrogen. Her body shape changes. She grows taller, her breasts develop and hair starts to grow under her

▶ We learn to read from about the age of five. Reading gives us another way to learn about the world about us.

arms and between her legs. She also starts to menstruate, as her ovaries start to release one egg each month.

A boy also gains height rapidly at puberty. His testes start to produce the hormone testosterone.

Girls are fully grown by the age of 16 years.

▼ This sequence shows how rapidly boys' and girls' bodies change as they grow up.

baby   toddler   child   adolescent (at puberty)   young adult

▶ It is important to stay fit and healthy no matter what your age. Swimming is one activity for people of all ages.

He grows hair under his arms, on his face and between his legs, and his voice gets deeper. His penis and testes enlarge and begin to produce sperm.

New skills

As children, we learn to read and write. We also develop important social skills, such as how to co-operate with others and make friends. Learning continues throughout our lives. When we leave school and go to work, we must learn new skills to do our jobs. We must also learn how to organize our time and money. Later we may learn to care for our children and teach them the things we have learned.

Growing older

By the age of about 20, the human body is fully developed. Muscles are in peak condition and so is the brain.

Gradually a person's body starts to age. No one can explain exactly why. Although our cells are renewed throughout our lives, it seems that over time our genetic code becomes less precise and more mistakes creep in. Our skin starts to wrinkle, and our eyesight and hearing become less sensitive. Older people tend to have slower reactions and do not resist disease so well.

key words

- growing
- life expectancy
- puberty
- skills
- socializing

Boys are fully grown by the age of 18 years.

| young adult | adolescent (at puberty) | child | toddler | baby |

FIGHTING DISEASE

Our waterproof, protective skin keeps out most of the millions of unwanted bacteria and viruses that try to invade our bodies every day. Even if the skin is cut or the intruders get in through the nose or mouth, our immune system provides an army of defenders ready to deal with them. Failure can mean disease and illness.

The skin is not only a physical barrier, it also has an array of chemical weapons to help fight invading germs. Oil from the skin contains substances that kill bacteria, and inside the nose, sticky mucus traps and destroys invaders we inhale. Ears contain wax to do a similar job, and the stomach produces a chemical cocktail of acid to kill bacteria we eat with our food.

ALLERGIES

Like all our body systems, the immune system is finely tuned. Sometimes a person may become so sensitive to an everyday substance that they develop an allergy to it. Dust or pollen, for instance, may be dealt with like dangerous invaders as the body launches an all-out attack. Pollen grains can cause hay fever, which is a typical allergic reaction. Sufferers develop red, itching eyes, a runny nose and often sneeze uncontrollably. Some foods, including peanuts, contain chemicals that produce a severe allergic reaction in some people that has to be treated in hospital.

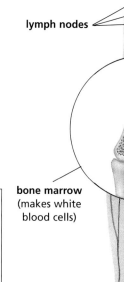

► Hazel trees produce vast amounts of pollen which can affect some hay fever sufferers in spring.

tonsils

thymus gland

spleen

lymph nodes

bone marrow (makes white blood cells)

▲ The lymph system produces antibodies and white blood cells in the spleen and lymph nodes. The lymph nodes, or 'glands', swell up when you have an infection. The thymus gland and the tonsils also help fight infection.

 key words

- antibodies
- defence
- hay fever
- illness
- lymphocytes

In the 1990s the World Health Organization estimated that 80 per cent of the world's children were being vaccinated against diphtheria, tetanus, polio and tuberculosis. These diseases have killed millions of children in the past.

IMMUNIZATION

Immunization is a way of preparing the body to fight serious diseases. When you are given a vaccine against a disease, a tiny amount of a bacterium or virus is allowed to enter your body. This triggers your immune system, which produces antibodies and memory cells that will protect you against the disease for many years.

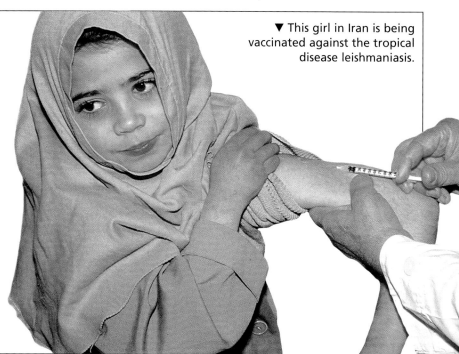

▼ This girl in Iran is being vaccinated against the tropical disease leishmaniasis.

Next line of defence

A cut in our skin is like a door into the body for invading germs. Damaged cells release a substance called histamine that causes redness and swelling. The redness causes a slight increase in temperature, which helps to kill bacteria. Blood vessels widen and white blood cells leak out of them and move into action.

White blood cells and antibodies

We have several different types of infection-fighting white cells in the blood. Two of the most important are lymphocyctes and macrophages. Lymphocytes produce special chemicals called antibodies to fight bacteria and viruses. Each invader is slightly different, and each antibody is exactly matched to destroy just one type. Macrophages engulf the dead and dying bacteria and viruses and slowly digest them.

Some antibodies and some special memory cells stay in the blood after we have recovered from an infection. The memory cells quickly alert the immune system and step up antibody production if we meet the same invader again.

▼ The bone marrow produces both lymphocytes and macrophages. It produces thousands of different kinds, each effective against a different disease. When an invader gets into the blood, millions of copies of the cell that is effective against that invader are produced.

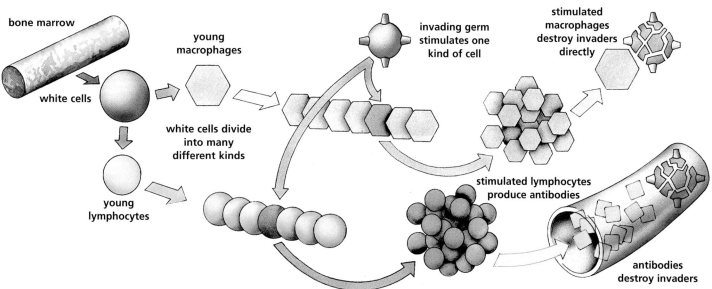

bone marrow

young macrophages

invading germ stimulates one kind of cell

stimulated macrophages destroy invaders directly

white cells

white cells divide into many different kinds

young lymphocytes

stimulated lymphocytes produce antibodies

antibodies destroy invaders

KEEPING HEALTHY

London in the middle of the 19th century was a filthy and unhealthy place. Sewage found its way into rivers and into the drinking water. In 1858 – in what is known as the Great Stink – the River Thames became so smelly that Members of Parliament fell ill. They decided to build an underground sewage system for the city.

By the end of the 19th century people in Britain and other wealthy countries were living much longer, healthier lives. A clean water supply was one of the main reasons why.

In poorer countries clean water is still one of the most pressing health needs. Water contaminated by sewage spreads diseases such as cholera, typhoid, dysentery and river blindness. And across the world more people die each year from malaria than any other disease, and mosquitoes, which carry malaria, breed in stagnant water.

key words

- cholesterol
- fitness
- sewage
- vaccination

▼ These people in West Africa are being given a pill to prevent river blindness. The medicine kills the parasites before they can damage a person's eyes.

▲ Senior marathon runners show how regular exercise keeps the heart and muscles fit and healthy.

Diet and exercise

Conditions in the environment can have a huge impact on your health. But the way you live also makes a big difference. A healthy diet and lots of exercise are vital for good health.

For a balanced diet, you need to eat foods that give you energy, and build up your strength, but vitamins, minerals and fibre are also important. A shortage of vitamin C, for example, reduces the body's ability to fight infection.

Healthy hearts

Many deaths in the developed world are caused by heart attacks. Being overweight can cause high blood pressure and make it harder for the heart to pump. Regular exercise reduces the risks of heart disease.

Prevention is better than cure. Vaccination programmes have succeeded in getting rid of smallpox, reducing deaths from polio and saving thousands of people's lives.

SNEEZES AND DISEASES

Every time you sneeze, millions of water droplets and germs shoot into the air at the speed of a racing car. People around you breathe the germs in. This is one of the ways in which coughs and colds spread rapidly from person to person.

Infections of the nose, throat and chest are among the most common of all diseases. But other diseases, such as heart disease and cancer, are not caught from other people. They are usually caused by the way we live, the genes we have inherited from our parents, by what we eat, or by chemicals in the environment.

Infectious diseases

The germs, or bacteria and viruses, that can make us ill reach our bodies in many different ways. They can enter through the air we breathe, from dirty water or food, or from contact with animals or insects that carry diseases.

We pick up infections such as chickenpox several days before they begin to affect us. This time is called the incubation period, when viruses are multiplying inside us. Then the itching spots, which are symptoms of the disease, appear. They are the body's reaction to the chickenpox viruses. Gradually, our immune system kills the viruses, and we recover.

Sometimes, so many people are affected by the same infection at once that an epidemic develops. Influenza, or flu, epidemics occur every few years, as new strains of influenza virus emerge. Today, epidemics can spread from country to country quickly, as air passengers take the virus with them as they travel around the world.

▲ Although we cannot see them, millions of bacteria and viruses fly out every time we sneeze. Flu, pneumonia and tuberculosis can all be spread in this way.

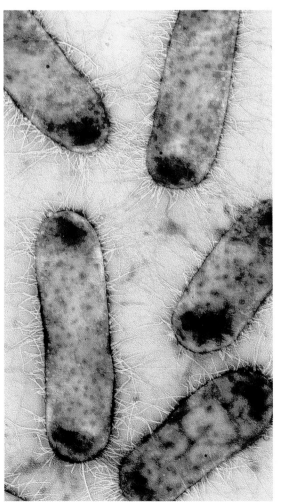

◄ These bacteria are called *E. coli*: they occur naturally in our digestive systems. Some strains of *E. coli* can cause vomiting and diarrhoea if they are eaten with food.

key words

- bacteria
- epidemic
- infection
- malaria
- viruses

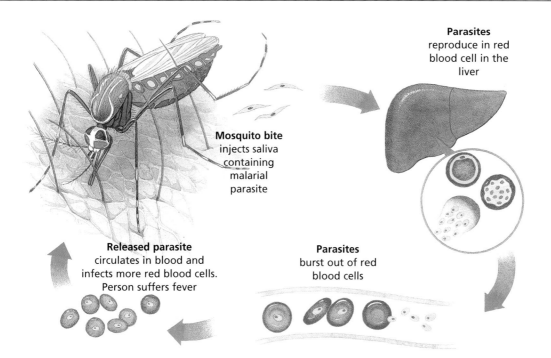

Parasites reproduce in red blood cell in the liver

Mosquito bite injects saliva containing malarial parasite

Released parasite circulates in blood and infects more red blood cells. Person suffers fever

Parasites burst out of red blood cells

◄ The lifecycle of a malarial parasite. When a mosquito bites a human, it injects saliva containing the parasite. The parasites reproduce inside red blood cells, then burst out into the blood. The new parasites infect more red blood cells, and the person suffers from fever.

Some people are thought to have caught CJD (Creutzfeldt-Jakob Disease) from eating beef from cows infected with 'mad cow disease', or BSE (Bovine Spongiform Encephalopathy).

Viruses

Viruses can only reproduce inside other living cells. They cause many diseases, from cold sores to rabies. Each of these viruses affects different cells in the body. Human immuno-deficiency (HIV) viruses affect the white blood cells that help us fight infections. People who carry the virus become less able to fight off minor infections. If the damage to their immune systems becomes very severe, it may result in Aids (Acquired Immune Deficiency Syndrome).

Parasites

Malaria is a disease that kills more than 3 million people every year. It is not caused by bacteria or viruses, but by a tiny parasite that lives in the blood. The parasites are transferred from person to person by mosquitoes.

LOUIS PASTEUR

Louis Pasteur (1822–1895), a French chemist, was the first person to realize that diseases are caused by germs. In 1881 he successfully found a vaccine for anthrax, a fatal disease of animals. The Pasteur Institute in Paris was founded in 1888 to investigate rabies. It is now one of the world's most famous centres of medical and biological research.

Many other parasites can live on or in our body. They come in many different shapes and sizes. Some of the largest are tapeworms, which live and feed in our intestine. Our most common parasites are tiny mites which feed on dead skin cells under our nails and even in our eyelashes.

▼ Victims of the plague being taken for burial in the 14th century. Almost a third of Europe's population died of plague in the 1300s. Bacteria carried from person to person by rat fleas are the cause of plague.

COPING WITH CANCER

Cells in our bodies are always dividing, as new cells replace old ones. But sometimes the process goes wrong, and a cancer cell is formed. Cancer cells divide rapidly and form growths called tumours. They can spread to take over a whole organ and stop it working properly. If cells break away from the tumour, they can travel to other parts of the body and start new tumours.

We do not know why some people get cancer while others don't, but faulty genes are certainly the cause of some cancers. Others are caused by chemicals in the environment, or by germs.

 **key words**
- chemotherapy
- smoking
- tumour

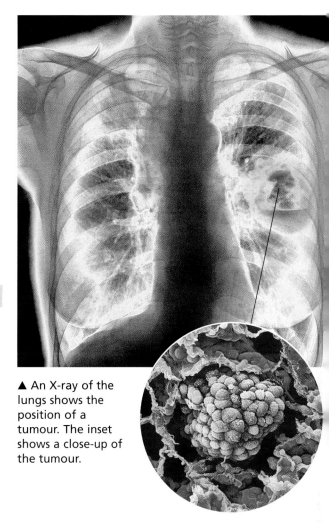

▲ An X-ray of the lungs shows the position of a tumour. The inset shows a close-up of the tumour.

Different cancers

Cancer is not a single disease – different cancers can affect almost any part of the body. The most common types affect the digestive system and lungs. In women, cancers of the breasts and cervix (the neck of the womb) are also common.

Smoking is the cause of almost all cases of lung cancer. Tobacco smoke contains chemicals called carcinogens, which irritate the delicate linings of the lungs. The more cigarettes a person smokes, the greater

▼ Radiotherapy is a type of cancer treatment which uses radiation to kill cancer cells. A narrow beam of radiation is focused directly at a tumour so that the healthy cells nearby are not damaged.

their risk of suffering from lung cancer. Fortunately, the risk of getting cancer is reduced when someone stops smoking.

Cancers of the skin are also quite common. Many types of radiation, especially ultra-violet rays from the Sun, can damage skin cells and cause cancer.

Cancer treatment

Most cancers can be treated successfully if they are caught early enough. Some treatments involve surgery to remove the tumour. This is often followed by a course of strong drugs (chemotherapy). Many of these drugs have unpleasant side-effects because they kill healthy cells as well as cancer cells.

In the most up-to-date treatments, drugs are delivered directly to the cancer cells using 'magic bullets'. These are special antibodies which only attach themselves to cancer cells.

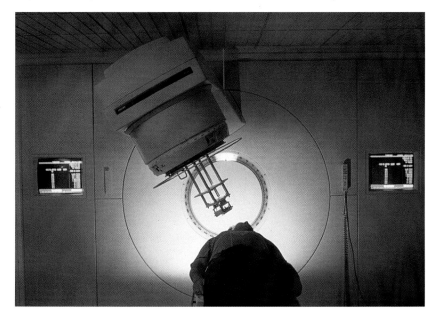

TREATING ILLNESS

In the past, doctors were too expensive for ordinary people, who would visit a barber, a tooth-puller or a herbalist for treatment. A barber would be happy to do minor operations as well as haircuts. There were few effective treatments for illnesses, and people died of diseases which are easily cured today. One of the most popular cures was applying leeches to suck blood from the patient.

Today we understand much more about how the body works and what causes illness. Diagnosis – a doctor's assessment of what is wrong with a patient – has become much more accurate. Advances in technology have led to new equipment and better treatment.

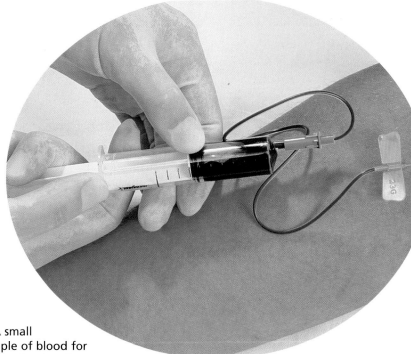

▶ A small sample of blood for testing is taken from a vein in a patient's arm using a syringe.

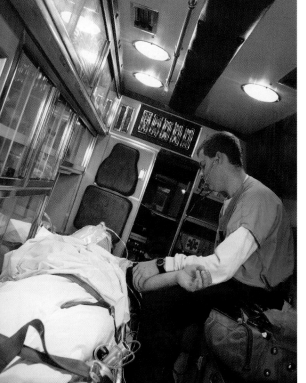

◀ Paramedics are specially trained to give emergency treatment in well-equipped ambulances as a patient is being taken to hospital.

Accurate diagnosis

Doctors still use simple ways to find out what is wrong. A view inside the mouth can reveal signs of infection, and unusual blood vessels in the eye can be a sign of the disease diabetes. Stethoscopes, first used in 1816, magnify the body's breathing and heart sounds so that the heart and lungs can be checked.

Doctors can also take samples of urine and blood, and send them for testing. Such tests can reveal the presence of bacteria and other substances, which help to pinpoint what is wrong.

Technical support

Advances in technology mean that many babies born prematurely (early) have a good chance of survival. They are kept in incubators where nurses care for them. Special sensors monitor the baby's breathing and heart beat.

Patients who are seriously ill may go into an intensive care unit. Here, artificial ventilators can take over their breathing, while tubes deliver drugs directly into their bloodstream. Sensors monitor the patients all the time, checking their breathing and heart rate through electrodes connected to their chest.

key words

- antibiotic
- incubator
- intensive care
- stethoscope

Clean and safe

Medical equipment must be clean and free of germs. Most surgical instruments, such as scissors and forceps, made of stainless steel, can withstand being sterilized. Most are sterilized in a device known as an autoclave, which heats them to over 100 °C. Many everyday items such as gloves and sterile syringes are made of disposable plastic, which is hygienic and can be thrown away.

▶ A machine used for analysing blood samples. Such machines can carry out a whole range of tests on a small sample of the patient's blood. The results of the tests help the doctor to diagnose a patient's illness.

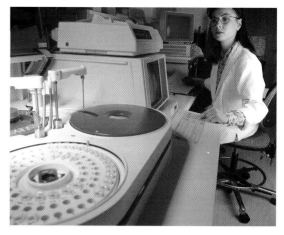

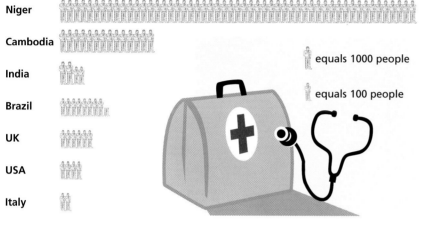

Number of people per doctor

Niger

Cambodia

India

Brazil

UK

USA

Italy

equals 1000 people

equals 100 people

▲ This graph shows the number of people per doctor in different countries. In developed countries such as the USA, most people have access to a doctor. But in places like Niger, in Africa, there is only one doctor for every 53,000 people.

Medicines and cures

Drugs and medicines are used to cure diseases or to relieve symptoms. Most traditional remedies relied on herbs. Modern drugs are produced and refined in large factories, although many were first discovered from natural sources. Aspirin, for example, came from the bark of a willow tree.

One of the most important medicines discovered in the 20th century was antibiotics, which kill bacteria. The first to be found was penicillin.

▼ A medical centre in Venezuela. Such centres mean that people living in remote areas can get vaccinations and other medical support.

Complementary medicine

Complementary medicine means any treatment that isn't one of the standard, traditional treatments used by most doctors. Here are some examples.

Acupuncture is an ancient Chinese therapy that stimulates nerves by inserting needles through the skin. It can be used as a treatment or as an anaesthetic for certain operations. Aromatherapy treatments use fragrant plant oils and massage to treat many conditions from strains to cancer. Homeopathy is a form of treatment in which patients take tiny doses of substances that produce similar symptoms to their illness.

Health centres

Today, patients can be treated with painkillers, antibiotics and a full range of other drugs. Some doctors and patients prefer a combination of these medicines with older treatments such as acupuncture and homeopathy. Doctors who work in health centres may have the support of physiotherapists, chiropodists, nurse practitioners and herbalists to treat their patients.

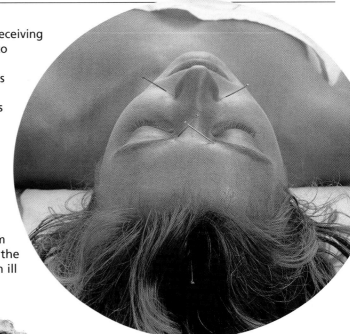

► A woman receiving acupuncture to the face. Acupuncturists believe that there are lines of energy criss-crossing the body. By inserting needles into the skin at points where energy lines cross, they aim to re-balance the energies of an ill patient.

HIPPOCRATES

Hippocrates was the most famous doctor of ancient Greece. He was born around 460 BC. He understood that sickness was due to natural causes, rather than evil spirits or star signs, and that patients might recover if they rested, exercised, and ate proper food. Today, doctors take an oath in which they promise to help their patients. This is called the Hippocratic oath.

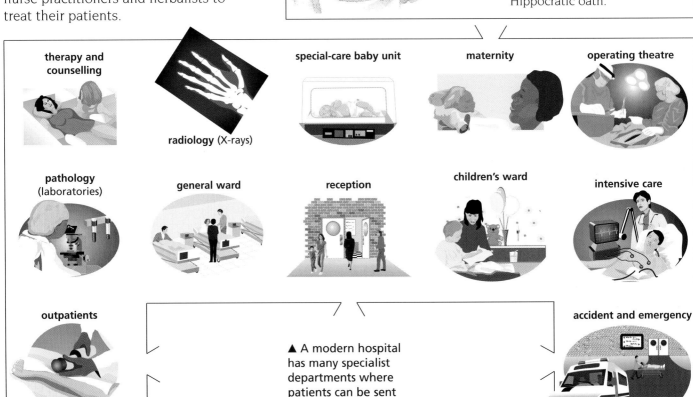

therapy and counselling

radiology (X-rays)

special-care baby unit

maternity

operating theatre

pathology (laboratories)

general ward

reception

children's ward

intensive care

outpatients

▲ A modern hospital has many specialist departments where patients can be sent for the treatment they need.

accident and emergency

LOOKING INSIDE THE BODY

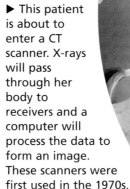

U ntil the 20th century, doctors had to guess what was happening inside the body from what they could see or feel from the outside. Now a mother can see her baby's heart beating and watch its limbs moving, long before it is born.

Ultrasound scanners are used in most hospitals to check a baby is developing well. They show the valves of the heart as it beats and even the sex of the baby.

X-rays

An important milestone for medicine was the discovery of X-rays in 1895 by the scientist Wilhelm Röntgen. X-rays were used to look at broken bones for the first time in 1896 and are still used in hospitals almost every day.

CT scanners

CT (Computerized Tomography) scanners are X-ray machines controlled by computers. They send out a succession of

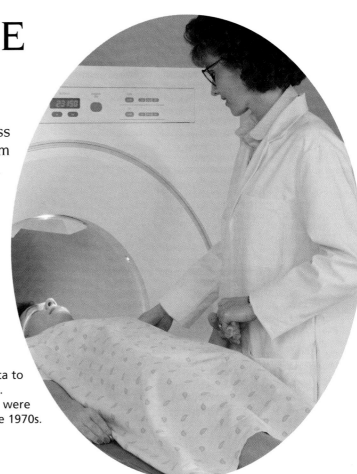

▶ This patient is about to enter a CT scanner. X-rays will pass through her body to receivers and a computer will process the data to form an image. These scanners were first used in the 1970s.

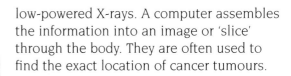

key words
- ultrasound
- X-ray

◀ MRI pictures can be coloured to reveal abnormalities of the brain. In this picture you can see the eyes in their sockets and the folded cerebral hemispheres.

low-powered X-rays. A computer assembles the information into an image or 'slice' through the body. They are often used to find the exact location of cancer tumours.

Magnetic resonance imaging

Magnetic Resonance Imaging (MRI) uses radio waves and magnets to produce images. Fatty tissues show up brightest, and MRI scanners are used to examine nerves and the brain. They can check conditions such as multiple sclerosis, which affects the nervous system.

Another way to look at the brain is a technique known as PET (Positron Emission Tomography). The patient swallows a liquid that contains tiny amounts of radioactive substances. These substances accumulate in certain parts of the body, which show up in scanner pictures. The technique is so sensitive that it can identify a person who is suffering from depression from an image of the brain.

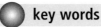

DELICATE OPERATIONS

Until the 19th century, all operations were carried out without an anaesthetic. Even pulling out a tooth could be unbearably painful. Patients had to be held or strapped down and surgeons had to work fast. Drugs such as alcohol and opium dulled the pain, but patients had to be brave.

The use of ether, chloroform and nitrous oxide, the first true anaesthetics, began in the 1840s. Since then, surgery has developed enormously. Today, before a major operation, patients are given a drug to relax them, then an anaesthetic to make them sleepy or unconscious. For small operations such as having a tooth out, a local anaesthetic is used to numb part of the body.

During some operations, especially those involving the heart, a patient's whole body may be cooled down by ice. As the body's temperature falls all the body's systems slow down. This reduces the risk that the brain will be damaged by a lack of blood or oxygen.

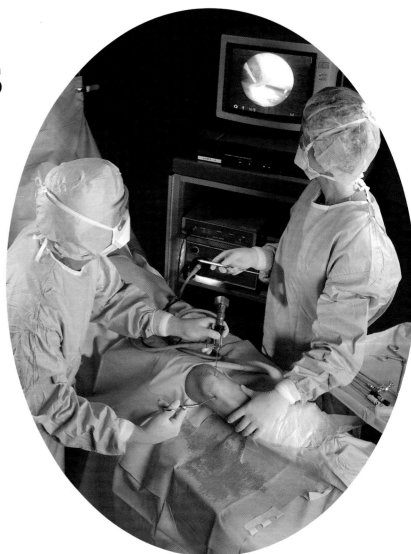

▲ Keyhole surgery. Doctors watch on a screen what they are doing inside the patient.

Keeping clean

Another problem with surgery before the 19th century was infection. Harmful bacteria or other germs got inside the patient's body during the operation, and the patient died of disease. In modern operating theatres every surface and every surgical instrument is sterilized (all bacteria are removed). The clothes and gloves that the surgical team wear are also sterile.

◀ In this picture of 16th century surgery you can see the patient praying and being held down by the doctor's assistant as his leg is cut off. Hot irons are being used to cauterize or seal the wound.

Keyhole surgery

Usually an operation involves making a large cut in the body. Keyhole surgery is a new technique that allows surgeons to perform operations through a small hole. An endoscope, a thin, flexible tube with a light and a camera at the end, is pushed in through a hole in the skin. The endoscope is guided by remote control, and surgeons follow what they are doing on a screen. Endoscopes with special attachments, such as scissors, forceps or a cutting laser, can be used for simple operations.

Transplants and spare parts

Bone marrow, hearts, lungs, kidneys and the cornea of the eye are just a few of the many body parts that can be transplanted. In a transplant, a damaged or diseased organ is replaced by a healthy organ from someone else, often someone who has been killed in an accident. A few organs, such as kidneys and bone marrow, can be transplanted from living donors.

Sometimes artificial organs can be used to replace weak or damaged body parts. Hip and knee joints can be replaced with plastic or metal substitutes, and artificial eye lenses can be implanted after an operation to remove a cataract.

key words
- anaesthetic
- blood transfusion
- endoscope
- hip replacement
- operating theatre

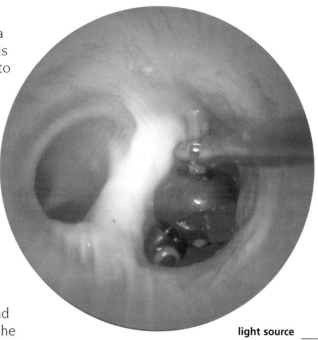

◄ This photograph shows an endoscope removing the top of a martini stirrer that has got stuck in the patient's trachea (windpipe).

▼ The parts of an endoscope.

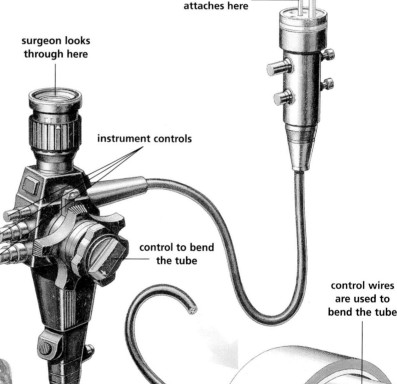

surgeon looks through here

light source attaches here

instrument controls

control to bend the tube

control wires are used to bend the tube

tiny surgical instruments can be inserted down this channel

fibre optic cables take light through the tube

JOSEPH LISTER

When Joseph Lister (1827–1912) was Professor of Surgery in Glasgow in the 1860s, he became concerned about the number of patients whose wounds became infected after operations. He had heard about Pasteur's discovery of bacteria, and decided that bacteria might be causing the infections. So he started to use carbolic acid as an antiseptic. He sprayed it into the air, and soaked his instruments, his patients' skin and his own hands in it. It was unpleasant to use but it worked. The number of infections and deaths fell dramatically. Antiseptic surgery spread rapidly and operations finally became safer.

GLOSSARY

The glossary gives simple explanations of difficult or specialist words that readers might be unfamiliar with. Words in *italic* have their own glossary entry.

absorption The process by which one substance is taken in by another. The nutrients from food are absorbed into the blood after digestion.

anaesthetic A drug given to a patient about to undergo an operation. Anaesthetics dull pain and may make the person unconscious for a short time.

antibiotic A drug, for example penicillin, that destroys *bacteria* or prevents them from growing.

antibody A protein produced by the blood as a defence against harmful *bacteria*.

artery A blood vessel which carries blood from the heart to other parts of the body.

bacteria Microscopic one-celled organisms. Some are useful but a few can cause diseases such as meningitis, tetanus and pneumonia.

bladder A muscular bag which collects urine from the kidneys and stores it until it can be released.

cancer An uncontrolled growth of cells in an organ of the body which develops into a *tumour*.

cell The basic unit of living things.

chromosome A structure made up of *genes*, which carries genetic information.

digestion The process by which food is broken down into tiny parts which can be absorbed by the blood.

DNA (deoxyribonucleic acid) The chemical which makes up *genes*.

enzymes Chemicals which speed up vital processes such as digestion.

evolution The gradual change in an organism over many generations.

fertilization The fusion of an egg and a sperm. After fertilization, the egg can begin to develop into a baby.

genes The parts of a *chromosome* which contain the code for characteristics that are passed on from parent to offspring.

haemoglobin The red substance found in red blood cells. Haemoglobin carries oxygen around the body.

hormones The body's chemical messengers. They control many processes, such as growth and reproduction.

immunization Giving a person protection against a disease, usually by *vaccination*.

infection A disease that is caused by germs.

intestine The long tube in which food is *digested*.

kidney One of the two bean-shaped organs which filter the blood and produce urine.

liver The body's largest organ, which controls the level of sugar in the blood, processes toxins and produces bile.

nerves Bundles of nerve cells which carry electrical messages to and from the brain and spinal cord.

neuron A cell that is part of the nervous system and sends electrical messages to and from the brain.

puberty The time when the body's reproductive organs become active. Boys and girls change to become young men and women.

reproduction The production of offspring by two parents, in which a male and a female sex cell join together.

skeleton A strong framework that supports an animal's body.

sperm The male sex cell, which joins with the female sex cell to produce offspring.

tumour A swelling caused by an irregular growth of cells which have no useful function. There are two types of tumour, benign and malignant. Malignant tumours, or *cancers*, may spread to other parts of the body.

vaccination Injecting a substance into the blood so that it produces *antibodies*, which provide protection against a particular disease.

vein A blood vessel which carries blood from the body back to the heart.

virus Microscopic organisms, smaller than *bacteria*, which reproduce by infecting living *cells*. Chickenpox, colds and influenza are all caused by viruses.

vitamins A group of substances found in food, which are necessary for good health.

womb The organ inside the body of a woman, and other female mammals, in which the fertilized egg grows and develops into a baby.

INDEX

Page numbers in **bold** mean that this is where you will find the most information on that subject. If both a heading and a page number are in bold, there is an article with that title. A page number in *italic* means that there is a picture of that subject. There may also be other information about the subject on the same page.

A

absorption 13, *15*
acupuncture *42*
adolescence *32*, 33
adrenal glands *21*
adrenaline 20, 21
ageing 33
AIDS (Acquired Immune Deficiency Syndrome) 38
allergies 34
alveoli *16*
amniotic sac *31*
anaesthetics 42, 44
anthrax 38
antibiotics 41, 42
antibodies *34*, 35, 39
antiseptics 45
anus *12*, 13
aromatherapy 42
arteries *18*
aspirin 41
asthma 16
axon *22*

B

babies **30–31**, 32, 40, *43*
bacteria 13, 34, *37*
    antibiotics 41
    digestive system *37*
    immunization against 35
    infectious diseases *37*, 40, 44, 45
balance 23, *24*
bile 14
birth 30, **31**, 40
bladder *6*, 8, 15
blindness *25*
blood *6*, **18–19**
    blood pressure 36
    blood vessels 7, 13, 17, *18*
    cells 19, *34*, 35, 38
    donors *19*
    manufacture 8, 14, 19, *34*
    nutrients in 12, *15*
    oxygen supply 17, 18, 19
    sugar (glucose) 14, *20*, 21
    testing for disease 40, *41*
body language 28
bones *6*, **8–9**, 10, *13*
    bone marrow 8, 19, *34*, 35, 45
    joints 8, 9, 45
    skeletons *4*, *8*, *9*
Braille *25*
Braille, Louis (1809–1852) 25
brain *6*, 8, 10, *18*, **22–23**, 24
    emotions 27
    memory 26
    scan *43*
    sleep 27
    speech and language 28
breasts 32, 39

breathing 9, 15, **16–17**, 23
bronchitis 16

C

cancers 37, **39**
capillaries 17, *18*
carbohydrates 10–11, *12*
carbon dioxide 16, *17*, 18
carcinogens 39
cataracts 45
cell division 7, 39
cells *6*, 7
    ageing 33
    blood *19*, *35*
    brain 26
    damaged 35
    egg 30
    nerve (neurons) *22*, *23*, 26
cerebellum *23*
cerebrum *23*
cervix *31*, 39
chemotherapy 39
chickenpox 37
cholera 36
chromosomes *29*
circulatory system *6*
cochlea *24*
colds 37
colon *12*
colour blindness 29
colour vision 24, 29
communication 5, 28
co-ordination *23*, 32
cornea *25*, 45
corpus callosum *23*
CT (Computerized Tomography) scanners *43*

D

defence system 34
dendrites *22*
depression 43
diabetes 21, 40
diagnosis 40, *41*
diaphragm *16*, *17*
diet 10–11, 16
    and health 36, 37, 42
digestion 9, 10, **12–13**, 14
diphtheria 35
diseases 14, 20, **34–39**
    and ageing 33
    epidemics 37
    genetic 29, 37
    heart 19, 36, 37
    immune system 34–35, 37
    immunization 35, 36, 38
    incubation period 37
    infectious 37, 44, 45
    lung *16*
    water-borne 36
DNA (deoxyribonucleic acid) 29

doctors 40, 41, 42
    surgeons *44*, 45
dreaming 27

E

ears *24*, 34
E. coli (*Escherichia coli*, bacteria) *37*
eggs 21, 29, 30, 32
electrical messages 6, 22, 24
emotions 27
endocrine glands 20, *21*
endorphins 27
endoscopes *45*
enzymes *12*
epidemics 37
excretory system *6*
exercise 33, *36*, 42
eyes 24, *25*, 45

F

fallopian tubes *30*
farming 5
fats 10–11, *12*, 14
fertilization 30
fibre optics *45*
fingerprints 7
fire *4*
fleas 38

G

gall bladder *14*
genetics *6*, **29**
genetic diseases 29, 37, 39
germs 34, 35, *37*, 38, 41, 44
    see also bacteria and viruses
glands 13, **20–21**
    lymph nodes 34
    thymus 34
glucose 14, *20*, 21
goitre *20*
growth and development 12, 20, 21, **32–33**

H

haemoglobin 19
hair *7*, **32–33**
hay fever 34
healthy lifestyle 11, **36**
hearing 23, *24*, 28
heart *6*, 8, 9, 10, *14*, **18–19**
    adrenaline 21
    beat 19, 20
    disease 37
    exercise 36
    surgery 44
    transplants 45
heart attacks 19, 36
herbalists 42
Hippocrates (born about 460 BC) *42*
histamine 35
HIV (human immuno-deficiency virus) 38
homeopathy 42
Homo erectus 4
Homo habilis 4
Homo sapiens 4, 5
hormones 20–21, 27, 32–33
hospitals *42*
human beings 4–5

Human Genome Project 29
hygiene 41, 44, 45
hypothalamus 21

I

ileum 13
illness 34–35
immune system 34–35, 37
immunization *35*, 36, 38
incubators 40, *42*
infections 19, 44, 45
inheritance 29
insulin 20, *21*
intensive care 40, *42*
intestines 8, *12*, 13, *14*
iris *25*

J

jaundice *14*
jaw 8, *13*
joints *8*, *9*, 45

K

kidneys *6*, 14, **15**, 21, 45

L

language 5, 26, **28**
larynx *28*
lasers 45
learning 23, 26, 32, 33
leeches 40
lens *25*
lips 7, 28
Lister, Joseph (1827–1912) *45*
liver 14, 15, 20
lungs *6*, 8, **16–17**, *18*, 19
lung cancer 39
lymphocytes 35
lymph system 34

M

macrophages 35
Magnetic Resonance Imaging (MRI) 43
malaria 36, *38*
medicine 40–42
    anaesthetics 42, 44
    antiseptics 45
    chemotherapy 39
    complementary (holistic) 42
    diagnosis 40, *41*
    drugs 39, 41, 42, 44
    hygiene 41, 44, 45
    intensive care 40
    radiotherapy 39
    surgery 39, *42*, **44–45**
    vaccination 35, 36, 38
melanin 7
memory 23, 26
menstruation 32
milk 10, 21, 31
    pasteurization 38
mind 26–27
minerals 10–11, *12*
mosquitoes 36, *38*
mouth *12*, *25*, *28*, 34
movement 6, **9**, 22, *23*, 32
    reflex 23
mucus 17, 34

muscles 6, 7, **8–9**, 10, *20*
 cardiac 19
 contraction *9, 12*, 19
 diaphragm *16, 17*
 exercise *36*
 peristalsis *12*
 reflex *23*
 touch sensors 25

N

nails 7
Neanderthals *5*
nephrons 15
nervous system *6, 7, 9, 13,*
 22–23
 brain 26
 spinal cord *6, 22, 23*
neurons *22, 23*
nose *6, 16, 17,* **25**, 34
 infections 37
nucleus *6*

O

oesophagus 13
oestrogen 21, 32
operating theatres 44
organs 6, 8, *14*, 30
 see also brain; heart; kidneys;
  liver; lungs; stomach
 artificial 45
 cancers of *39*
 sense 24
 sex *30*
 transplants 45
ovaries *21, 30, 32*
oxygen *6, 16, 17,* 18, 19

P

pain 25, 27
pancreas *12,* 13, *20, 21*
paramedics *40*
parasitic diseases *38*
pasteurization 38
Pasteur, Louis (1822–1895) *38*, 45
pathology *42*
penicillin 41
penis *30,* 33
peristalsis *12*
pituitary gland *21*
placenta *31*
plague *38*

plasma 19
pneumonia 37
polio 35, 36
pollen *34*
pollution 16, *17*, 37, 39
Positron Emission Tomography
 (PET) 43
pregnancy 20, 21, 30
primates *5*
progesterone 21
proteins 10–11, *12,* 14
puberty 20, *32, 33*
pupil *25*

R

rabies 38
radiology *42*
radiotherapy *39*
rectum 13
reflex *23*
reproduction *6,* **30–31**
genes and chromosomes 29
reproductive glands *21*
respiration *6,* 16
retina 24, *25*
ribs *8, 16, 17*
river blindness 36
rods and cones 24
Röntgen, Wilhelm (1845–1923)
 43

S

saliva *12,* 38
semicircular canals *24*
senses *23,* **24–25**
seratonin 27
sewage 36
sexual intercourse 30
sexual maturity 20
sight *23,* 24, *25*
 colour blindness 29
skeletons *4, 8, 9*
skills (learning) 33
skin 7, 34
 ageing 33
 cancer 39
 touch sensors 25
 wounds *7, 19,* 34, 35
skull *8*
sleep 27
smallpox 36
smell 25

smoking 16, 19, 39
sneezing *37*
sound waves *24*
speech 23, 26, **28,** 32
sperm 21, 29, *30,* 33
spinal cord *6, 22, 23*
spleen *34*
starvation 11
sterilization 41, 44
stethoscopes 40
stomach *12,* 13, *14,* 34
sugar 13, 14
sunlight *7, 24, 39*
surgery 39, *42,* **44–45**
 anaesthetics 42, 44
 keyhole 44, 45
 transplants 45
sweat *7, 15, 20, 21*
synapses 22
synovial fluid *8*
syringes 40, 41

T

taste *23,* 24, 25
tears 27
teeth *12, 13,* 28, 44
testes *21, 30, 33*
testosterone 21, 32
tetanus 35
throat 25, 37
thymus gland *34*
thyroid gland *20, 21*
tissues *6*
tongue *12, 25,* 28
tonsils *34*
touch *7, 23,* 25
tuberculosis 35, 37
tumours *39*
twins *29*
typhoid 36

U

ultrasound scanning *43*
ultraviolet light *7, 39*
umbilical cord *30, 31*
urea *14,* 15
urine *14,* 15
 testing for disease 40

V

vaccination *35,* 36, 38

vagina *30, 31*
veins *18*
villi *13*
viruses 34, 35, *37,* 38
vitamins **10–11,** *12,* 14, 36
vocal cords *28*
voice box *28*

W

waste products *6, 12,* **13, 15,**
 16, *18*
water 15
windpipe *6,* 16, *17,* 28
womb *30, 31*
World Health Organization
 (WHO) 35, 36
wounds *7, 19,* 34, 35

X

X-rays *42, 43*

ACKNOWLEDGEMENTS

Key
t = top; c = centre; b = bottom; r = right; l = left;
back = background; fore = foreground.

Artwork
Black, Brad: 41 c. **Courtney, Michael:** 18 tr.
D'Achille, Gino: 38 c; 45 bl. **Frank Kennard:** 8 tl; 22
tr. **Full Steam Ahead:** 24 b. **Hawtin, Nigel:** 42 b.
Hook, Richard: 46 b. **Hiscock Karen:** 40 tl. **Learoyd,
Tracey:** 10 b. **Parsley, Helen:** 23 b; 26 tr, b; 27 b; 28
b (John Martin & Artists); 32–33 b. **Sarson, Peter:**
45 br. **Saunders, Michael:** 9 br; 12 bl; 13 t; 17 tl; 18
b; 20 b; 22 b; 24–25 c; 28 tr; 30 b; 31 c; 35 b.
Sneddon, James: 10 tr. **Visscher, Peter:** 4 tl; 7 tl; 10
tl; 12 tl; 14 tl; 15 tl; 16 tl; 18 tl; 20 tl; 22 tl; 24 tl; 26
tl; 28 tl; 29 tl; 30 tl; 32 tl; 34 tl; 36 tl, 37 tl; 39 tl; 43

tl; 44 tl. **Weston, Steve:** 6 b; 7 b; 8–9 c; 8 bl; 14 tr;
15 br; 16 b; 21 c; 23 t; 34 tr. **Woods, Michael:** 38 t.

Photos
*The publishers would like to thank the following
for permission to use their photographs.*

Corbis: 6 tr; 7 tr (Joseph Sohm; ChromoSohm Inc.);
23 tr; 27 t; 29 tr (Picture Press); 33 tr (Carl Corey);
36 tr (Joseph Sohm; ChromoSohm Inc.); 40 bl; 41 tr;
43 tr, bl; 44 tr.

Oxford Scientific Films: 5 tr (C. W. Helliwell); 11 tr
(Paul Kay); 17 br (Mike Hill).

Photodisc: 25 br (Scott T. Baxter).

Science Photo Library: 4 tr (John Reader); 11 bl
(James King-Holmes/Northern Foods); 13 bl
(Biophoto Associates); 14 bl; 15 cl (Scott Camazine);
16 tr (Mark Clarke); 19 tl (Dr Yorgos Nikas); 19 bl
(Jerry Mason); 19 bl (BSIP VEM); 20 tr (John Paul
Kay, Peter Arnold Inc.); 21 br (Mark Clarke); 29 bl
(CNRI); 30 tr (D. Phillips); 31 bl (Keith/Custom
Medical Stock Photo); 32 tr (Mark Clarke); 35 tr (A.
Crump, TDR, WHO); 34 bl (Dr Jeremy Burgess); 36 b
(A. Crump, TDR, WHO); 37 tr (Matt Meadows); 38 b
(Jean-Loup Charmet); 37 bl (Eye of Science); 39 tr
(Simon Fraser); 39 cr (Moredun Animal Health
Ltd.); 39 bl (BSIP LECA); 40 tr (Saturn Stills); 41 b
(Jan Bradley); 42 tr (Tim Malyon & Paul Biddle); 44
bl; 45 t (Alexander Tsiaras).